The Harmon Killebrew Story

Harmon Killebrew started playing baseball when he was eight. In high school he was one of the greatest all-around athletes. Shortly after graduation, at seventeen, he signed a bonus contract with the Washington Senators. He spent several years on the Washington bench and in the Senators' farm system because several major league managers recognized his potential as a hitter, but were not convinced he could make the grade as a fielder, runner or thrower. Only Calvin Griffith, President of the Senators, had faith in him and Harmon surprised the league in 1959 by becoming one of the Senators' most feared sluggers. In his quiet way Harmon Killebrew, now with the Minnesota Twins, has assumed leadership of the team, and there is little doubt that someday his name will be emblazoned in baseball's Hall of Fame.

At 17, Killebrew becomes the first bonus player in the history of the Washington Senators, 1954.

With his mother and wife in Griffith Stadium, 1959.

Harmon with Ted Williams, Boston Red Sox outfielder, 1959.

A handshake from President Eisenhower before the start of the Boston-Washington game, with Calvin Griffith, president of the Senators, looking on, 1959.

Injured while running out a ground ball, Killebrew is helped off the field by trainer George Lentz and Elmer Valo. Manager Cookie Lavagetto at the right, April 15, 1961.

A safe slide into home as Cleveland catcher John Ramano grabs the throw during sixth inning of the American League game, Sept. 27, 1961.

Killebrew follows through on his swing connecting for a double in the third inning of Minnesota Twins-Washington Senators game, May, 1962.

Killebrew crosses home plate and shakes hands with Jimmy Hall after his third inning homer, June, 1963.

Killebrew makes good his promise to hit a homer for Johnny Guiney, 9, when the boy was hospitalized with severe burns. Johnny with his idol, Sept. 12, 1964.

Killebrew with former home run king Roger Maris before the start of the game between the Minnesota Twins and the New York Yankees, 1964.

Hank Greenberg and Harmon Killebrew with the Sultan of Swat crowns presented at the Maryland Professional Baseball Players Association's Tops in Sports banquet, 1965.

A sad moment for Manager Sam Mele when Killebrew flied out in ninth inning of third World Series game, 1965.

THE
HARMON
KILLEBREW
STORY

by
Hal Butler

JULIAN MESSNER
NEW YORK

Published by Julian Messner
Division of Pocket Books, Inc.
8 West 40 Street, New York 10018

© Copyright 1966 by Hal Butler

Photographs used with the permission of Wide World Photos

Printed in the United States of America
Library of Congress Catalog Card No. 66-14005

The Harmon Killebrew Story

1

Clark Griffith, eighty-four-year-old president of the Washington Senators, sat at his desk and shuffled hopelessly through a batch of scouting reports on the club's minor league prospects. He was wondering vaguely where he would find a ballplayer talented enough to lift the Senators out of the American League's second division when the door to his office opened and a handsome gray-haired man walked in. Griffith's thin, wrinkled face broke into a smile of recognition.

"Well, if it isn't my good friend Herman Welker," he said. "What do you have for me this time? A ballplayer, I hope."

The Honorable Herman Welker, United States Senator from Idaho, sat down in a nearby chair.

"That's exactly what I have for you, Griff," he said. "The best ballplayer in the world!"

Griffith's alert eyes sparkled. He was quite aware that Senator Welker considered himself a knowledgeable baseball scout, but "the best ballplayer in the world" sounded a little exaggerated to him.

"The last time you were here," Griffith said patiently, "you were boasting about how you discovered Vern Law, an Idaho boy, for the Pittsburgh Pirates. You know what I said then, don't you?"

"Sure," said Welker. "You said you hadn't seen a good Idaho player since the great Walter Johnson, and you asked me when I was going to find you another like him."

"And now you have?"

"Right. Only this one's not a pitcher, he's an infielder— and a whale of a hitter."

Griffith permitted his gaunt frame to settle deep into his swivel chair. He folded his bony hands over his stomach and regarded his friend with affection.

"Who is this great player?" he asked.

Senator Welker leaned forward in his enthusiasm. "He's just the best ballplayer you ever saw, that's all. He's better than Mickey Mantle right now!"

"That's going pretty far."

"Well, he's every bit as good a slugger as Mantle," Welker insisted.

"Yes?"

"He hits as long as Mantle."

"Yes?"

"And he can throw better than Mantle."

Griffith's eyebrows raised in doubt. "How old is he?"

"Seventeen," said Welker. "Near eighteen."

Griffith picked up a record book on his desk, flipped some pages, and ran his finger down a column of statistics. "Let's see," he mused. "Last year, 1953, Mantle hit two ninety-five, had twenty-one home runs and batted in ninety-two. The year before that he hit three eleven. This year is only his fourth in the majors and he looks like a great one who can't miss. And you say this seventeen-year-old kid is better than Mickey?"

"Well," the Senator hedged, "if he isn't better now, he *will* be. This kid weighs almost two hundred pounds, has a real set of shoulders on him, and he can hit a ball ten miles."

"Nine miles," said Griffith drily, "would be adequate." He put the book aside and gazed levelly at his friend. "All right, Herman. We'll take a look at this phenom of yours. Where can we see him?"

"You'll have to go to Payette, Idaho. He's playing semipro ball for Payette in the Idaho-Oregon Border League."

Griffith touched a buzzer on his desk and when his secretary came in he said, "Get Ossie for me." A moment later Ossie Bluege, formerly a star third baseman for Washington and then farm director for the Senators, stepped into the room.

"Ossie," Griffith said, "I want you to fly to Payette, Idaho, and take a look at a ballplayer Senator Welker says is the best he's ever seen. He's supposed to hit better than Mantle, throw better than Mantle, and I guess do everything better than Mantle."

Bluege grinned. It was early in the 1954 season and the Washington Senators had finished in the second division for the last seven years.

"If he's that good," he said, "we can use him."

Griffith looked with mock sternness at Senator Walker. "It's a long way from here to Idaho," he said, "and I swear that if Ossie makes the trip out there for nothing, I'm never again going to take your advice on a ballplayer. Is that understood?"

Senator Welker nodded. "I'll promise never to darken your office again, Clark, if this boy doesn't measure up."

"Okay. And now, maybe you ought to give us this kid's name, eh?"

"His name," said Welker, "is Harmon Killebrew."

Payette, Idaho, five years earlier in the summer of 1949: Harmon Killebrew, thirteen years old, bounced on the seat of the big enclosed truck and listened to the rattling and banging of the metal milk cans in the back. They had just picked up the cans of milk from the farmers outside of Payette and in a few minutes they would be unloading them at the Farmers' Co-op in town. Lugging around the big ten-gallon cans of milk was hard work, but Harmon was happy with his summer job and the opportunity to earn his own money.

Carl Swigart, the truck driver, turned in at the Co-op building and carefully backed the truck up to the loading dock. He looked down at Harmon and winked.

"Think you got enough strength left to unload the cans?" he asked slyly.

Harmon nodded vigorously. "Sure," he said. "I can handle them. You don't have to worry about me."

Swigart continued to appraise him as Harmon descended from the truck cab, went around in back and climbed the four steps to the loading platform.

"We'll have 'em off in no time," said Harmon, wanting to assure the driver that he was capable of handling the job.

The truck driver grinned. "You're a pretty husky kid at that," he remarked. "Where'd you get your muscles?"

"From my dad, I guess," said Harmon seriously.

"The way I hear it," said the driver conversationally, "all the Killebrews were husky. Wasn't your dad a wrestler at one time?"

"Yes, sir. He's pretty strong, my dad. And I guess my grandpa was too."

. . . It was true. Before Harmon was born, two generations of Killebrews had become famous for their strength and athletic achievements. Harmon's grandfather, Culver Killebrew, was reputed to have been the strongest man in the Illinois detachment of the Union Army during the Civil War and the heavyweight wrestling champion of the Northern forces. His father, Harmon Clayton Killebrew, Sr., had been a bruising fullback for West Virginia Wesleyan and Millikin College in Illinois and had received honorable mention on one of Walter Camp's All-America teams. Following his football career, he had wrestled on the Pacific Coast before moving to Payette in 1922, where he first took a job as sheriff and, later, as a house painter. Harmon's mother was the former Katherine Pearl May, whose ancestors, while not noted for prodigious strength, were nevertheless rugged enough to carve out a living in primitive Pike County, Illinois, in the early days of the western movement.

Into this sturdy family young Harmon was born on June 29, 1936, and his arrival occasioned no particular excitement in the sleepy town of Payette on the Idaho-Oregon border. Payette in 1936 had a population of just over two thousand people, and its nearest claim to fame was the fact that it was located fifteen miles from Weiser where the Hall of Fame pitcher, Walter Johnson, was discovered. Beyond that, Payette, Idaho, was an unlikely place for a coming big league baseball player to be born. . . .

Harmon struggled gallantly with the heavy milk cans and the driver helped him unload them. As soon as all the cans were unloaded Harmon knew he would be free, and then, after dutifully reporting home first, he would join the kids on the high school baseball field. Somehow, the diamond seemed to be his element, a place where he felt at home. He had been playing baseball since the third grade, when, as an eight-year-old, he was barely able to lift a big Louisville Slugger. Now, at thirteen, he could swing the bat pretty well— heredity had given him a good set of arm muscles and jobs like hauling milk cans had helped to develop them.

When Harmon and the driver had finally unloaded the last can, Swigart took out a handkerchief and wiped sweat from his forehead.

"I guess that does it, Harmon," he said. "You've put in a good day's work. You better go home and get a good nap."

Harmon looked startled. "Oh, I couldn't do that!"

"No? Why not?"

"I gotta play baseball," said Harmon. The next instant he was off on a trot toward home, leaving Swigart shaking his head at the stamina of youth.

By the time Harmon reached the ball field a group of boys had gathered. As young Killebrew approached, one of them shouted, "Here comes Harmon now! That makes it even so we can choose up sides!"

Harmon trotted up to the gathering of boys at home plate. Already two of the boys were "choosing up" with a bat, one fist over the other until the boy whose hand ended on top got first pick.

"I'll take Harmon," said the winner promptly.

"Nuts!" said one of the other boys in disgust. "That makes two good hitters on the same side. It ain't fair."

"I got first choice, didn't I?"

"Yeah. I suppose."

"Well, then why shouldn't I take Harmon?"

"Okay, okay! You got 'im!"

Harmon stood on one side, pawing the dirt with his foot, embarrassed over the argument about his services. Invariably he was the first to be selected, because he was the most muscular boy in the group and the one with an ability to hit the ball a long way.

The game was played in the hot afternoon sun. Harmon's team won, and young Killebrew was one of the reasons. He collected several long hits, including a home run that he ran out furiously as the outfielders chased down the ball, and as he walked home after the game one of the boys asked him, "Harmon, did you ever think of being a big league ballplayer when you grow up?"

Harmon laughed. It sounded ridiculous.

"Big league ballplayer? Fat chance! For one thing, I wouldn't be good enough, and besides, who would ever find me out here in Idaho?"

"They found that other guy."

"Who? Walter Johnson?"

"Yeah."

Harmon grinned sheepishly. "I'm no Walter Johnson," he said.

Harmon Clayton Killebrew was the youngest of four children born to Clay and Katherine Killebrew. When he was thirteen years old his eldest brother, Gene, was already thirty; his sister, Eula, was twenty-four; and his other brother, Bob, was fifteen. Consequently, his closest companion during his boyhood years was Bob, only two years his senior. But the entire Killebrew family was close-knit, and his sports-minded father, particularly, took an interest in the fact that Harmon showed every indication even at an early age of becoming a good ballplayer. Not only did he play baseball on the vacant lots of Payette at every opportunity, but he also received his first taste of organized ball as a Knot Hole baseball player while he was in grade school.

But what set Harmon apart from others was his intense dedication to the game and his desire to improve himself. While many boys were content simply to play the game, Harmon would practice for hours in the backyard of his home at 726 North Seventh Street, swinging a bat at imaginary pitches. One day he got into trouble trying to perfect his swing. He noticed that a rose on one of the family rose bushes was just about waist-high—greatly resembling a belt-high ball down the middle of the plate. Harmon swung his bat, hit the rose squarely, and scattered the petals on the ground.

Then he observed a rose on the bush that was shoulder-high. He swung again and smashed the flower to bits. It was just when he was swinging at a knee-high rose that he heard his mother's anguished cry.

"Harmon! What are you doing to my roses?"

Young Killebrew received a spanking for his bit of mayhem, so that the next time he would know the difference between a rose and a baseball.

When Harmon finished grade school and enrolled at Payette High School in 1950, his father urged him to become active in school athletics.

"If you can make it in high school athletics," he said, "you've got something extra. Sports will build your body and mold your character. And it will teach you the value of cooperation and teamwork."

"I suppose I could try out for baseball," Harmon said, a little dubiously. "I like baseball."

"Fine," said his father. "But try out for football and basketball too. That way you'll learn where your skills really lie, what your best game really is."

Harmon followed his father's advice. Immediately upon enrollment in the fall of 1950, he went out for football. His brother, Bob, was already a star halfback, and Harmon joined him in the Payette Pirates' backfield, playing both halfback and fullback. At that time he weighed 155 pounds and was about five feet six inches tall.

Aided by advice from his more experienced brother, Harmon did passably well in his freshman year, and in the 1950–51 basketball season he joined Bob again on the cage team. In basketball, too, Harmon showed promise with accurate shooting and an ability to grab rebounds. Then, in the spring, the two brothers got together on the same baseball team, Bob playing left field and Harmon shortstop. As a baseball player Harmon raised some eyebrows among the coaches and the spectators, for even at the tender age of fourteen he showed promise as a long-ball hitter.

By the time the 1951 football season came around, Bob had graduated. Harmon was now on his own. There was no longer a brother act, and Harmon knew he would have to make the grade by himself.

He started out well. Early in September the Payette High School Pirates, in the Snake River Valley Conference, played a tune-up game with the Caldwell Cougars, a Big Six Conference team. They were 40–0 underdogs. But they lost by only a 26–19 score, with young Harmon keeping them in the game with several key passes for long gains. This would have been an encouraging start for both Harmon and the team except for one thing—Killebrew suffered a serious injury to his knee in the game, which put him out of action for the season.

Coach Walter Buettgenbach shook his head sadly. "It's too bad," he said. "Harmon looks like the best prospect we've had at Payette High in quite a spell."

That winter Harmon went to a hospital in Boise for surgery on his knee. The operation kept him out of basketball awhile and although he returned to the squad late he was not up to par and the team finished in the cellar.

By spring, though, Harmon's knee was again in good shape, and he immediately began to make his mark on the Payette Pirates baseball team. Playing third base, Killebrew emerged in his sophomore year as a top hitter, consistently going two-for-three and three-for-four at bat. His slugging helped the Pirates win the Snake River Valley Conference title.

That was just the beginning. Payette High's football fortunes also took an upturn in the fall, and Harmon had a lot to do with it. New coach Jack Dailey installed the stocky Harmon at the quarterback slot and he proved to be a good passer, a smart signal caller and an effective punter. His leadership sparked the team to a run for the title, and late in the season the Pirates met the Nyassa (Oregon) Bulldogs in a key game for the Snake River Valley Class A Conference Championship.

It was a tough hard-fought game. Neither team scored in the first quarter as they probed each other for weak spots. Calling the signals, Harmon tried everything, but a stout Bulldog defense stopped the Pirates on the ground. With their line plays smothered and their end sweeps turned in, Harmon took to the air in the second quarter.

The teams were at midfield. Using the split T formation, Harmon took the snap from center and faded for a pass. He spotted Jim Davis, a high school All-American end, on the forty-five-yard line and lobbed a pass to him. Davis went all the way for the touchdown. Killebrew tried the point after touchdown but it went awry. Score: Pirates 6, Bulldogs 0.

Fighting back, the Bulldogs drove to a touchdown in the third quarter; and when they missed the point, the score was tied at 6–6. Then, in the fourth period, the Pirates got a break. The Bulldogs fumbled on their own one-yard line and the Pirates recovered.

With four downs to make a yard, it looked like a cinch— but it wasn't. Killebrew handed off to his fullback for a try at the line, and the Bulldogs stopped the play cold. Twice more the Pirates drove at the center of the line, but the Bulldogs held. On fourth down and still a yard to go, Harmon tried the quarterback sneak. He tucked the ball in his stomach and bulled over for the TD. Then he passed to end Jim Davis for the extra point. The game ended Pirates 13, Bulldogs 6.

Having won the conference title in both baseball and football, Payette High School—and Harmon Killebrew—suddenly found themselves the talk of the town. During the 1952–53 season the basketball team also made a run for the championship. Under Coach Millard Reynolds, Killebrew became a consistently high scorer and the team prospered. But the title eluded them; they finished second.

As a junior in the spring of 1953, Harmon again swung the big bat on the Pirates baseball team. He hit .419 and led the team to another SRV title.

The 1953 football season was less successful, however. Harmon injured his leg in a preseason nonconference game and was out of action for two weeks and ineffective for longer than that. During this time the Pirates lost five straight games. It wasn't until the last game of the season, against the Nyassa Bulldogs again, that Killebrew flashed his best form. That day he was virtually a one-man team. Harmon carried the ball 21 times and averaged 9.5 yards per play. He threw 13 passes and completed 7 for 204 yards. He ran back two kickoffs for touchdowns, traveling 80 yards each time, scored two more TDs on plays from scrimmage, passed for three scores and intercepted an enemy pass for a TD. With extra points, he scored 34 points that day in a 60–32 win over Nyassa.

"It was Harmon's last game," said Coach Jack Dailey, "and he sure made the most of it."

The 1953–54 basketball season was a fiasco for everyone but Harmon. The Pirates finished sixth in the seven-team league, but Killebrew placed second in the league in scoring with 189 points, a game average of 15.75. At the end of the season Killebrew was selected as the Most Valuable Player in the SRV Basketball League.

The spring of 1954 was Killebrew's last high school baseball season before graduation, and he made the most of it. He hit .375—the only Pirate hitter over .300—and led the team in slugging with two home runs, a triple and a double among his hits. The Pirates again won the title. During award ceremonies at Payette High at the end of the season, Coach Jack Dailey called Harmon, a twelve-letter winner in three sports, "the greatest athlete I have ever coached." His football jersey, No. 12, was retired and placed on permanent display in the hall of the school.

Harmon's high school days had been happy ones, for he excelled not only in athletics but also in his studies. When he graduated it was with a B-plus average. But one tragic event occurred to sadden his junior year in high school— his father, who had taken such a keen interest in his athletic success, passed away.

It was a severe blow to the Killebrew family, for it left Mrs. Killebrew with the lonesome job of shepherding the family over the crisis. Gene, the oldest son, was now putting out a weekly newspaper in the nearby town of Plymouth. Bob was with the Army in Korea. And young Harmon, trying to do his bit to help the family financially, took a summer job as a maintenance worker for Payette High School. And as he worked he dreamed of a future that might include either a professional baseball or a college football career.

Both were distinct possibilities. In his last two years at Payette High he was closely watched by baseball scouts. The Boston Red Sox had scout Earl Johnson checking him out in his junior and senior years, and the Brooklyn Dodgers had scout Bill Smulich doing the same. In addition, the New York Giants and Cincinnati Reds had local bird dogs on his trail.

At the same time, he was being offered athletic scholarships at several western colleges, notably the University of Oregon. Both Don Kirsch, the baseball coach, and Len Casanova, the football coach, were interested in the young man's talents.

"I just don't know what to do," Harmon said to his mother one day. "I feel I ought to be earning some money to help out the family. But even though there are a lot of scouts looking at me, nobody has made me an offer yet."

"Well," said Mrs. Killebrew, "a baseball career could be

profitable. But a college education is a valuable thing to have. Maybe you ought to take the scholarship offer at Oregon."

Troubled, Harmon talked to Casanova again. The Oregon football mentor urged him to go to college.

"You'll never regret a college education," he said. "Sure, you might sign with a big league club, but you'd probably knock around in the minors for four or five years and—who knows?—you might not even make the grade. The way I look at it, you can play baseball for Kirsch and football for me on a scholarship, get your education, and at the same time develop enough skill in sports so that if you do sign a professional contract you'll have a much better chance of making the grade."

"I'll think it over, Mr. Casanova," Harmon said. "It's something I have to think about a long time."

By the time Killebrew—called Killie by his friends—graduated from Payette High School in the spring of 1954, he was already playing sandlot baseball for the Payette Packers in the semipro Idaho-Oregon Border League. He was now a squat, husky young man tipping the scales at close to 190 pounds. His thick-set body was balanced upon two short legs and his height was at that time about five feet nine. He played shortstop most of the time, and he was something less than a gazelle in the field. But when he swung a bat there was every likelihood that the ball would land in the next county.

Playing with a semipro outfit whetted Harmon's appetite for baseball. He was now seventeen years old, approaching eighteen in June, and he reasoned that if he spent four years in college, a possible two years in the service, and then three or four years in the minor leagues, he would be twenty-six or twenty-seven years old before he got a chance in major league baseball. That, he thought, was much too late to start a big league career. Still, there was no denying the value of a college education. It was a puzzling problem.

Aside from his family and sports there was only one other

love in Harmon's life—an attractive young Mormon girl named Elaine Roberts who had been his sweetheart since the seventh grade. She was aware of Harmon's dilemma too, and often she and Harmon discussed the problem. But it always came down to the fact that Harmon would have to be the one to finally decide.

During this trying time, Earl Johnson of the Red Sox was the most persistent scout on the Killebrew trail, but he was handicapped in making Harmon an offer. The Red Sox had been a free-spending club for quite a few years, but recently they had clamped down on their bonus policy. A $6,000 limit had been set for signing a prospect, and this hampered Johnson in his negotiations.

"I'm going to try to do better than that by you, Harm," he said one day, "but it might take a little time. Will you promise me something?"

"I guess so."

"If any other offers come along, will you let me know before you sign?"

"I guess that's only fair," Killebrew said. "You've been the most interested of any in my career."

"Thanks, Harmon."

And it was shortly after that conversation that Ossie Bluege, of the Washington Senators, flew to Payette to see Harmon Killebrew play ball—and landed in a driving rainstorm.

2

Much to Ossie Bluege's disgust, the rains continued for three days, making baseball an impossibility. Harmon, always anxious for action on the diamond, began pacing the floor at home. He didn't know at the time that Bluege was pacing some himself. The scout began talking to men in town about Killebrew, and he found that everyone in Payette was high on the boy.

"I seen Killie play in his last three games," one of the men told him. "You won't believe it, mister, but that kid got eleven hits in thirteen times up in them three games. Four homers, two triples, a double and the rest singles. If that ain't hittin' the old apple, then I don't know what is!"

Bluege verified the story with Don Dibble, manager of the Payette Packers. The records showed he had hit six-for-six, three-for-three and two-for-four in his last three games. Eleven hits in thirteen times was exactly right!

"I've *got* to see this kid play," said Bluege to himself, "if I have to stay till Christmas!"

On the fourth night after Bluege's arrival the rain slackened temporarily. Since the entire town, including the Payette ball team, wanted to play so that Bluege could get a look at young Harmon, it was decided that a game would be started regardless of the weather. Before the game Bluege approached Harmon at the ball park and introduced himself.

"I'm glad to meet you," Harmon said. "I heard you were in town."

Bluege glanced up at the scowling sky. "It doesn't look like much of a night for a game," he said.

"Well, the field's muddy and it's still drizzling, but maybe we can get going," said Harmon hopefully.

The two walked to a nearby automobile and sat inside while the rain increased from a drizzle to a downpour. Finally Bluege made an impatient gesture.

"I don't think you'll ever get a game in tonight," he said, "and I'm afraid that other business is going to force me to return to Washington in the morning. Tell you what—why don't you fly to Washington and work out with the Senators? We'd be able to look you over then."

Harmon considered for some time, but at last he shook his head.

"I'd sure like to do it," he said, "but I don't think it would work. I guess I'll plan to go to the University of Oregon and get my education."

Suddenly the patter of rain on the car's roof stopped and players began to appear on the soggy field. Harmon was out of the car in a bound and heading for the diamond.

"Don't tighten up now!" Bluege called after him. "Just play your regular game."

"Yes, sir. I will, Mr. Bluege."

The Payette Packers used the high school diamond for their games, and on this night the field was in particularly bad shape. The long rains had turned the infield into a muddy swamp, and the grassy outfield was slippery and dangerous.

The Packers were facing a team from Emmett, Idaho, and the right-handed-batting Killebrew was up against Lynn

Moeller, a right-handed fast-ball pitcher. But neither this nor the presence of Bluege in the stands seemed to bother Harmon. Not that he wasn't anxious to do well, but he was by nature a calm and well-adjusted person and, besides, he had become accustomed to playing under the eyes of big league scouts. So he simply went about playing the game the best way he knew how—which turned out to be not bad at all.

Bluege saw him make a couple of errors on simple ground balls and winced a little each time. He also saw him make several good plays on the soggy infield, and on these occasions he smiled. But what he observed with more satisfaction than anything else was the way Killebrew was built. He was a mountain of a lad, and he made an impressive sight when he stood at the plate and waggled a bat threateningly at the pitcher.

What he did in his turns at bat was even more impressive. The first time up he flied out to deep left, but that was the only time the opposing pitcher got him out. The second time he stroked a line single into left field. The third time he rapped a long double off the right center field fence. And the last time he went all out, driving the ball on a line over the wooden left field wall.

Bluege's eyes popped. He nudged the man next to him.

"How far is that wall?" he asked.

"About four hundred feet," said the man.

"That drive must have gone four hundred and fifty then," said Bluege with a little awe in his voice.

"Every bit," grinned the man.

Bluege didn't stop to talk to Killebrew after the game. But the next morning he went to the outfield fence and paced off the distance between the wall and the spot where the ball had landed.

"Four fifty if it's an inch," he said with satisfaction. Then he called Clark Griffith. He could hardly keep the excitement out of his voice.

"I don't expect you to believe what I'm going to tell you," he said, and then proceeded to give Griffith a rundown on Harmon's accomplishments. He finished up saying, "For a seventeen-year-old kid, he *does* hit 'em like Mantle! And I'd say we'd better sign him—for a bonus—before somebody else gets to him."

Griffith ordered Bluege to offer Harmon a bonus of $30,000 —the first bonus ever authorized by the Washington club.

A bright sun pouring in the window awakened Harmon Killebrew the next morning. At first he turned in his bed, trying to get away from the brightness, but then he remembered that he had a job to do, and he bounced out of bed briskly and got dressed. In the kitchen he sat down to a breakfast of bacon and eggs.

"How did you do last night?" asked his mother.

"Three-for-four," said Harmon.

"I heard there was a scout from Washington in the stands."

"Yes."

"Did he talk to you?"

"Before the game, but not after," said Harmon, a little despondent.

Mrs. Killebrew sighed. "What are you going to do today?"

"Paint the high school gym," said Harmon practically. "It'll keep me busy and that gym sure needs a coat of paint."

After breakfast Harmon walked across town to the school and went to the gym where he had spent so many memorable hours during his high school days. The scaffolding was up and, mixing his paint carefully, he climbed up and began to apply it with long generous strokes to the wall.

While he was painting, an important meeting took place at his home. Ossie Bluege called shortly after he left and introduced himself to Mrs. Killebrew and Harmon's brother, Gene. As he entered the pleasant living room, Bluege noticed two Ted Williams bats standing in one corner.

"Where did Harmon get those?" he asked curiously.

"Earl Johnson of the Boston Red Sox gave them to him," said Gene. "He's been looking Harmon over for some time."

"Has he made an offer?" asked Bluege.

"Nothing firm," Gene said.

Bluege sat down in a comfortable chair. His face became serious.

"I saw Harmon play last night," he said. "I think he has a lot of potential, and the Washington club is ready to make him an offer."

Mrs. Killebrew glanced at Gene. She had great faith in her eldest son's ability to handle financial matters.

"We're willing to offer Harmon a bonus to sign," Bluege went on. "I think the offer will be attractive enough to appeal to him."

"There's just one thing," said Mrs. Killebrew quickly. "Harmon's got a scholarship offer at the University of Oregon. If he signed to play baseball he'd have to turn down a college education. That's turning down quite a bit."

Bluege agreed. "However," he said, "Harmon can always get his education in the off-season, if he wishes, and I think I can make the offer worthwhile. We're willing to give him thirty thousand dollars."

Again there was an exchange of glances. The figure was larger than either Mrs. Killebrew or her son had expected.

"That's pretty generous," admitted Gene.

"We'd break the figure down this way," pursued Bluege anxiously. "Six thousand a year in salary for three years and a twelve thousand dollar bonus split over three years. How's that?"

Mrs. Killebrew hesitated. "I've had no experience in negotiating a contract like this," she said. "What do you think, Gene?"

"Well, it's a very fine offer," Gene said, "and the family can use the money. I think Harmon should take it, although I'd suggest the contract be looked over by a lawyer first."

"By all means," agreed Bluege. "I'll draw it up and leave it at your lawyer's office."

At the high school gym, Harmon was still painting the wall when someone called up from the floor of the gym.

"Hey, Harmon!"

Killebrew looked down. It was his brother, Gene, and Don Dibble, coach of the Payette Packers, who had helped him so greatly to develop his baseball talents.

Harmon placed his brush carefully across the top of the paint can and descended to the gymnasium floor.

"What's up?" he asked.

"The Washington Senators just made you an offer," said Gene, smiling.

Harmon's heart jumped a little.

"Are you kidding?"

"No. They offered you thirty thousand dollars for three years."

The figure almost spun young Killebrew's head. That a big league club would offer him that much money to sign was almost too much for him to believe. He was only a semipro sandlotter, and $30,000 was an incredible amount of money, more money than he had ever dreamed of having.

"Bluege's leaving a contract at Senator Welker's law office," said Gene. "They'll look it over first before your mother signs it."

"And I want to be the first to congratulate you," said Don Dibble, holding out his hand.

Harmon shook hands with both Dibble and Gene. Then, suddenly, a thought struck him.

"I'll have to call Earl Johnson," he said.

"Why?"

"I promised that if anyone made an offer I'd let him know. So I'd better do it."

Back at home, Harmon called Johnson on the phone.

"I've got some news for you, Mr. Johnson," he said. "The Washington Senators just offered me some money to sign."

Johnson was instantly alert. "Who made the offer?"

"Mr. Bluege."

"How much did he offer you?"

"Thirty thousand dollars."

A low whistle came over the phone. Johnson knew that the Senators had never offered a bonus contract to a player before, so apparently they were strongly sold on Killebrew's potential.

"Did Bluege see you play?"

"Yes."

"How many games?"

"One."

"What did you do?"

"I hit a single, double and homer in four times."

"And I suppose he heard you had eleven-for-thirteen previous to that?"

"I guess so."

"That makes fourteen hits in the last seventeen times up," said Johnson with respect in his voice. "No wonder Bluege wants to sign you so bad!"

"Well, anyway," said Harmon, "I promised to let you know. What do you think I'd better do?"

Johnson sighed. He knew the Red Sox wouldn't offer Killebrew more than $6,000 to sign.

"Harmon," he said, "I have to be honest about this. That's a lot of money, and since I know I can't better it, I guess you'd better take it."

"Okay, then," said Harmon. "And thanks, Mr. Johnson."

That day the contract was written. The document was turned over to Senator Welker's Payette law office of Welker and Daniels, where legal minds pronounced it a good one, and Mrs. Killebrew signed the contract for the under-age Harmon.

And that was how young Mr. Killebrew came to Washington.

Harmon Killebrew sat at the window of the big airliner and gazed down on the sprawling metropolis of Chicago. The plane had been airborne for several hours, and now it was circling for a landing at Chicago's bustling Midway Airport.

The great city below him was a fascinating sight to Harmon. He had never been east of the Mississippi River, and having been born and raised in a small town he was not accustomed to the miles and miles of brick and concrete that made up a city such as Chicago. Besides, he had been on edge all day. It was June 22, 1954, and Harmon had not yet reached his eighteenth birthday. But here he was, in an airplane for the first time in his life, and flying to meet the Washington Senators, who were playing that day in Chicago.

It was too incredible!

He knew that Otto Bluege, brother of Ossie, was to meet him at the airport. He would be taken to a hotel, and later to famous Comiskey Park, and the very thought of walking out on a major league baseball diamond and taking practice with veterans who were already big names in the game was unnerving.

The plane nosed down and now Harmon could see the airport below. Seconds later they had touched down and were speeding along a landing strip, and he felt a slight tug at his body as the plane braked to a halt. Then it taxied in and the smiling stewardess opened the door.

Holding a small bag of belongings, Harmon emerged from the plane into the glistening sunlight. Slowly he made his way down the steps with the other passengers, and as he reached the bottom a gray-thatched man came forward to greet him.

"Harmon Killebrew?" he asked, holding out his hand.

"Yes, sir." Harmon shook the man's hand.

"I'm Otto Bluege. I've got a cab waiting."

Quickly they walked to the cab and a short ride took them to a hotel in Chicago's Loop. Otto Bluege ushered young Harmon into a hotel room where he was welcomed to the major leagues by several important men—Clark Griffith, president of the Washington club, Senator Herman Welker and manager Stanley Raymond (Bucky) Harris.

Harmon was given a warm reception and it made him feel good. But he was amazed when flashbulbs began to pop and reporters with poised pencils swooped down on him.

"What do they want to interview me for?" he asked Bluege in a puzzled tone. "I haven't even played a game yet."

"The price of fame," grinned Bluege. "You're the Senators' first bonus baby and that makes you news."

The questions came rapidly.

"What position did you play back home?"

"Do you know where you'll play with Washington?"

"Ever been to Chicago before?"

"Think you can hit major league pitching?"

Some of the questions were difficult, but Harmon tried to answer them all. Finally the ordeal was over and Bluege said, "I think maybe you and Bucky ought to have a talk."

Harmon and the Washington manager crossed to one corner of the room. Bucky Harris was a lean, wiry man with the worry creases of a big league manager in his face.

"Ossie was pretty impressed with you, Harmon," Harris said abruptly. "He says you're quite a muscle man."

"Well," said Harmon modestly, "I guess I just happened to be born with the muscles."

"I suppose you understand the bonus rule, don't you?"

"I think I do."

"It means that we can't farm you out to a minor league club for two years. We're going to try you out in some games, of course, but for the main part you're going to have to ride the bench quite a lot."

"I understand," said Harmon.

"Of course," Bucky went on, "you'll learn a lot as you watch. This team has a lot of nice guys on it, and they'll all try to help you and give you advice. Listen to them and learn. After all, they're pros and they know what this game is all about. I'll introduce you to the boys when we get to the park."

Get to the park! Famed Comiskey Park! Harmon could hardly wait to get a look at the giant stadium. When, a little later, he and Otto Bluege arrived at the park, Harmon got out and gazed up at its towering ramparts with awe. Without a doubt, this was the biggest sports arena he had ever seen. It seemed too large for the playing of a simple game like baseball.

Bluege led Harmon along corridors and down ramps until they came to a door with a sign in block letters that said "Visitors Clubhouse." Harmon walked in and stood silently for a moment, awed at the scene. It was a large dressing room with open-face lockers, a rubdown table, a caged office for the manager, and a lot of half-clad men getting dressed, snapping towels at each other, talking, shouting. The thought ran quickly through Harmon's mind: *These are big leaguers, honest-to-goodness real live big league ballplayers! And I'm a member of this team!*

Bluege guided the hesitant Harmon to Bucky's office, and

after another greeting by the manager he was introduced to a tall young man who clattered in on his spiked shoes.

"Harmon, this is Johnny Pesky," Harris introduced. "Johnny, our newest addition, Harmon Killebrew."

Harmon stood up and shook Pesky's hand. Pesky, he knew, held down second base for the Senators.

"You guys will bunk together on the road," Harris said. "And, Johnny, help the kid out. Explain the plays to him in the dugout. Let him have some of your experience."

"I'll sure try, Bucky," Pesky said.

Then Bucky took Harmon out and introduced him to most of the other players—Camilo Pascual, Eddie Yost, Roy Sievers, Jim Busby, Pete Runnels and others. Harmon was delighted that they all greeted him with warmth and seemed like a good bunch of fellows.

Eventually young Killebrew was fitted out with a uniform and walked through the tunnel to the Senators' dugout. As he came into the dugout from the rear, he saw the vast green field in front of him. It was his first sight of a major league ball park and it almost stunned him. Everything about it looked bigger—the diamond, the outfield, the stands. And everything about it looked smooth. The infield was manicured to perfection; the outfield grass looked like a putting green. He felt his heart pounding with excitement, and he thought, *It will even be fun sitting on the bench in parks like these.*

Young Killebrew took batting practice with the team that day, and Bucky Harris stood behind the batting cage and watched him through narrowed baseball-wise eyes. Harmon did nothing sensational with the bat, but he managed to hit a few towering flies to the outfield and a couple of line drives through the infield. At fielding practice, Bucky let him work out at shortstop—where he had played for the Payette Packers—and Harmon managed to handle what was hit his way, although not with any particular grace.

Bucky Harris turned to Coach Heinie Manush one time as Harmon whipped a throw to first.

"Good grief!" he exclaimed. "The kid throws like a girl!"

Ossie Bluege was standing nearby, and he wasn't going to permit such a remark about his protégé to go unchallenged.

"He throws like a quarterback, which he was," Bluege retorted. "Don't worry about him. He'll develop."

"I hope so," said Bucky. "But the way he looks now, he's three or four years away from the big leagues."

That day Harmon sat on the bench and watched his first major league baseball game—a close one in which the White Sox beat Washington, 7–5. Johnny Pesky talked to him as the play unfolded, explaining outfield throws and cutoff plays and all the other intricacies of the game. Harmon listened intently and learned that there was a great deal more to baseball than he had ever imagined in Payette!

The next day Harmon Killebrew again polished the bench with the seat of his pants. But before the game was hardly under way a milestone in Harmon's budding career occurred. As he sat and watched the Senators and White Sox battle it out, he was treated to a bit of managerial wizardry. Chuck Stobbs had started on the mound for Washington but wasn't effective. In the second inning, Bucky lifted Stobbs for a pinch hitter, Clyde Vollmer. Vollmer promptly got himself hit by a fast ball and limped down to first base. Harmon crouched forward on the bench, studying the play on the field with all the seriousness of a rookie wanting to make good, and wondering vaguely if he would ever get a chance to show what he could do.

"Killebrew!" It was Bucky Harris' voice.

Harmon almost leaped to attention.

"Yes, sir!"

"Go in and run for Vollmer!"

Harmon swallowed hard. His heart started to pound like a trip-hammer. How he ever managed to get off the bench and run out to first base he never knew—it was an automatic reflex that took over when his mind seemed paralyzed. All he knew was that suddenly he was standing at first base on a major league diamond and that his name—*his name*—was going to actually go in the box score!

Harmon glanced around quickly. Walt Dropo was the towering first baseman for the White Sox, and he looked to Harmon as if he were nine feet tall. There was the great Nellie Fox on second, experienced Chico Carresquel at short, Sherm Lollar behind the plate. And all at once the thought went through his mind, *What am I doing out here with these guys?*

Unfortunately—or perhaps fortunately—Harmon did not have to do anything on base. The next two batters lifted easy flies to the outfield to retire the side, and Harmon never had a chance to move away from the bag.

"Anyway, I can say I played in a big league game," Harmon said to Pesky when he returned to the bench, "even if I didn't do anything."

3

~~~~~~

The season turned out to be an extremely long and inactive one for Harmon. Bucky Harris tried his new rookie out in carefully selected spots, but he could not justify using him in place of his established veterans. As a result, Harmon spent a frustrating season mostly on the bench. In all, he appeared in just nine games, was at bat only thirteen times, had four hits and scored one run. His specialty with the Payette Packers—the home run—eluded him.

The season was also frustrating for the Senators as a team. They finished sixth, forty-five games out of first place, and their attendance dropped by 81,000 fans.

Bucky Harris gave Harmon permission to go home before the season actually ended so he could attend college, and when he returned to Payette he was greeted like a hero by his family and his high school sweetheart, Elaine Roberts. Harmon was his usual unassuming self as his family and friends congratulated him.

"Not much to crow about," he said. "I only played in nine games."

That fall two important events occurred in Harmon's life: he and Elaine became engaged, and Harmon entered the College of Idaho for the fall semester. When the semester ended, he spent the rest of the time at home, impatiently waiting for spring training to start in Florida.

Before it did, a shakeup occurred in the Senators' organization. The octogenarian, Clark Griffith, and his nephew Calvin, who had been adopted by the elder Griffith and made vice president of the club, decided that the sixth-place finish and the loss of fans dictated some changes. Bucky Harris was released as manager and his place taken by Charlie Dressen, a pepperpot of a man with some firm ideas about discipline. Harmon thought about the managerial change and decided it was relatively unimportant as far as his own future was concerned. He was only at the beginning of his career, and he would have to show something during spring training, no matter who was the manager.

"I hear Dressen's a taskmaster and gets the best out of his players," he said one day. "If he can get my best out of me, I guess it's all to the good." C634613 CO. SCHOOLS

Harmon reported to Tinker Field, the Senators' spring training camp in Orlando, Florida, knowing that he would be carefully scrutinized by Dressen. And he was. Dressen kept a wary eye directed at the young man from Idaho, standing behind the batting cage to evaluate his swing, and along the third base line as Killebrew played third, short and second during spring training. Although Dressen came to the immediate conclusion that Harmon had some potential as a hitter, he was greatly discouraged by his fielding. As a glove man, he left a lot to be desired at any position. He bobbled grounders, couldn't fade to his right or left fast enough, and his throwing arm was nothing to get excited about.

Harmon's sensitivities had been hurt when Bucky Harris made the comment that he threw like a girl, and they were injured again when the blunt-talking Dressen, exasperated at Harmon's inadequacies with the glove, snarled, "How do they expect me to win with guys like Killebrew?"

Harmon brooded about the remark for a while. "I guess I just don't have what it takes," he said to Pesky once. "Maybe I ought to quit and go back to Payette."

"None of that!" snapped Pesky. "You'll be all right. But not very many guys make the big leagues overnight. It's something you have to work at."

"I suppose," said Harmon, and went out the next day to work at it.

One day Dressen approached Ellis Clary, a Senator coach. "I want you to work with Killebrew," he said. "Hit him ground balls. Hit him a million of 'em. Make a glove man out of him."

Clary took to the assignment with a vengeance. "Harm, I want you to meet me out on the diamond two hours early tomorrow," he instructed. "I'm going to make a major league fielder out of you."

Harmon readily agreed. He was glad the Senator management was taking enough interest in him to offer him extra practice.

"I'll be here," he said.

The next morning Killebrew stationed himself at third base, and Clary slammed ground balls at him from home plate. Some were easy hoppers, others grass cutters that skimmed over the ground like bullets. Some went in the "hole" between third and short; others hugged the third base line.

The sun was out bright and hot. Killebrew felt himself sweating as he fielded the ground balls. Occasionally he had to stop to wipe his forehead. It was a rough, hard workout.

In addition to batting the balls, Clary appraised almost every play Harmon made. On one hopper Killebrew had a choice of coming in and fielding the ball on the short hop or dropping back to take it on a longer hop. He dropped back.

"No good!" snapped Clary. "You didn't play that ball right. You let the ball play you. Waiting for the long hop wasted time. If the runner was fast, you would have had to throw hastily—maybe a wild throw. Come in on those. Charge the ball. Grab it on the short hop and get your throw away."

Clary hit him several more just like it, until he had Harmon charging in on the ball and making the play properly.

Another time Clary drilled one to Harmon's left, the glove side. Harmon went to his left, somewhat awkwardly, but the ball skidded under his glove.

"You didn't get a jump on the ball," criticized Clary. "You waited too long, then lunged for the ball. Be on your toes, ready to go right or left at all times. Get the jump when the ball's hit and you'll have time to make a play like that."

On a smash just inside the third base line, Harmon went to his right, threw his glove across his body, knocked the ball down but did not hold it.

"You're going to have to learn to make that play," said Clary, and kept drilling him on this type of ground ball until Killebrew felt his legs weakening under the workout. When Clary finally let up on him, Killebrew came in smiling weakly.

"That sure was a workout!" he said.

"There'll be more like it, Harm," said Clary, not unkindly. "You know, we think you have great potential as a hitter. Your swing is a little awkward and you go for bad balls, but that should smooth out with experience. You *do* have power. All we have to do is teach you to field, throw and run."

"You make it sound like an awful tough job," said Harmon.

"Well, it might be. But I think you learn quick. Stick at it, kid, and don't give up."

There were many sessions with Clary after that, both in early practice meetings and in pregame drills, and although Dressen never commented about it, Harmon felt he was improving in the field.

All in all, Harmon did not have a particularly brilliant spring training, but because he was a bonus player and could not yet be farmed out, he went north with the team when they broke camp. The Senators were scheduled to play several games as they moved north, and during this interval Dressen caught Killebrew at his locker one day.

"I'm changing your roommate," he said.

Harmon just looked at the peppery manager. He liked Pesky and hated to lose him as a roomie, but it didn't matter so much that he was going to protest.

"I'm assigning Cookie Lavagetto to you," he said. "He's pretty high on you and I think he can help you."

"Thanks," said Killebrew, not knowing what else to say.

Cookie Lavagetto was a coach with the Senators, and as Dressen had said, he was as enthusiastic as Ossie Bluege about Harmon. He too saw great potential in the husky, square-shouldered young athlete, but he also knew the Killebrew weaknesses.

That night Harmon was lying on the bed in his hotel room when Lavagetto walked in. The coach took one look at him and threw a book on the bed.

"There, kid. Study that."

Harmon picked up the book, blushing a little as he saw what it was. It was a baseball rule book!

Lavagetto sat down and began to take off his shoes. He grinned at Harmon's reaction.

"You never get too old in this game that you can't read the rule book, over and over again," he said. "The more you know about the rules of the game, the more spontaneous your actions will be on the field when you're confronted with an unusual play. It's fine to know how to hit, and to field, and to run, and to throw. Those things are basic and you've got to learn 'em. I'll leave teaching you those things to Dressen and Clary. My job is to teach you to *think*."

Harmon grinned. "You might have the toughest job of all," he said, and the attempt at humor lightened the moment for the two men.

A few days later the Senators moved into Washington to open the 1955 season.

Opening day in Washington, D.C., is always a colorful event, with the President of the United States usually throwing out the first ball from a flag-draped box. On this occasion President Dwight Eisenhower did the honors, "The Star-Spangled Banner" was played as the players and fans stood at attention, and the roar of the crowd thundered down as the game got under way.

The color of the kickoff game thrilled Harmon Killebrew, and he was happy when his teammates won the opener from Baltimore by a lopsided 12–5 score. The Senators, despite their lowly standing in the league for many years, had some good players on the squad, and Killebrew learned a lot by watching and being with them. Players like outfielders Jim Busby and Roy Sievers, and infielders Eddie Yost, Pete Runnels and Mickey Vernon, were inspirations to him. Still he felt rather forlorn, sitting on the bench day after day with little hope that he would see action.

Lavagetto recognized the boredom Killebrew faced, and he did his best to keep Harmon's mind from growing stagnant. As the season progressed, Lavagetto kept up a running stream of chatter calculated to make Harmon think about the game.

"Okay," Lavagetto would say, "the score's two to one against us. Eighth inning. Man on first, nobody out. Does the batter swing or bunt?"

"He bunts the runner to second," Harmon would say.

Or, "Score's tied. Fifth inning. Man on first. Should he steal or play it safe?"

Or, "We're two runs behind. Good hitter at the plate. Two

men on. Two out. Count on the batter is three-and-one. Does
he take or does he swing?"

It was a little game they played, trying to outmanage the
manager, and Harmon learned a lot of "inside" baseball that
he hadn't known before.

Harmon didn't get to play much in the opening months of
the 1955 season. Occasionally he was called on to pinch-hit
or take a turn at third base in the late innings when the game
was either won or irretrievably lost—but that was all.

The season proved a dismal one for the club too. By mid-
June the Senators were threshing about like a fish out of
water. By June 24 they were mired deeply in seventh place.
They had lost six games in a row and fourteen out of their
last fifteen, and things had become so discouraging to the
desperate manager that Dressen decided to put Killebrew in
at third base and see what the youngster could do.

It was a Friday night game at old Griffith Stadium. The
weather was perfect. Still, only 4,188 fans showed up for the
game—and most of them had come to boo.

The opposition was the Detroit Tigers, and Billy Hoeft,
one of their top pitchers, was on the mound. Dressen placed
Killebrew's name in the number-seven spot.

"This Hoeft is plenty smart," said Lavagetto before Harmon took the field. "He's got a fast ball and a good curve.
But don't let him overpower you. Just stand in there and
take your cuts."

The game turned out to be a tragedy for the Senators.
The Tigers whipped them 18–7 for their seventh straight
setback. But for Killebrew it was a triumph.

In the second inning Killebrew grounded weakly to the
infield. No one else did much hitting either, and by the time
the fifth inning rolled around, the Washington Senators had
played a string of twenty-four innings without scoring.

"Maybe someday we might score a run," moaned Dressen in the dugout. "Then we'll pray for rain."

It was Killebrew's turn to bat. No one was on base. It was about the most relaxing situation in which a batter could step up to the plate, and Harmon decided he would stay relaxed and simply swing at anything that looked good.

Hoeft peered in for the sign. Killebrew had not batted often enough in the big leagues for pitchers to have any kind of "book" on him, so Hoeft decided to try him on a fast ball. It came in, cutting the heart of the plate—so fast that Harmon failed to offer at it.

Hoeft tested the young rookie with an outside and an inside pitch, but Killebrew wouldn't go for either. With the count two-and-one, Hoeft threw a slow curve that nipped the corner of the plate to even the count.

Harmon stepped out of the box, took a deep breath, and got back in. With two strikes on him, he had to protect the plate. He had to swing at anything that looked as if it would be called a strike.

Confident now, Hoeft tried for the strikeout with a fast ball. But he got it a little high and Killebrew clobbered it. The ball rose in a high arc toward left field and slammed into the twenty-fourth row of the bleachers—475 feet away!

It was Killebrew's first major league home run—and a dandy!

There was thunderous applause for the rookie as he circled the bases, and every hand in the dugout was out to be shaken.

"Nice goin', kid!" cried Lavagetto with delight.

"That's about as far as I've seen one hit out here!" yelled another teammate.

Dressen slapped Harmon on the seat of the pants and grinned at him. As for Killebrew himself, no thrill he had ever experienced in baseball equaled this. His heart had given a gigantic leap as the ball disappeared in the stands, and he was almost jittery with pleasure as he sat down in the dugout after touring the base paths.

But one baseball game—or one home run—doesn't make a career. Killebrew found, as the season went along, that he played only occasionally. He was used frequently as a pinch hitter, and he played a few complete games at third base. When the season ended he had participated in only 38 games, had 16 hits in 80 times at bat for a lowly .200 average, and had hit 3 more homers to bring his season's total to 4.

And the Washington Senators finished in last place.

During the fall of 1955 several things happened, in both Harmon's personal and baseball life, that had an impact on his career. On October 27, 1955, just one month before his eighty-sixth birthday, Clark Griffith, president of the Washington Senators, passed away—without living to see whether his $30,000 bonus gamble on Killebrew would pay off. The presidency of the Washington club was assumed by his nephew, Calvin.

In a reshuffling of managerial personnel, Charlie Dressen was given an office job in the club's scouting organization and Cookie Lavagetto replaced him as field manager. When Killebrew heard of the change, he said, "I get along fine with Cookie, so I'm glad for him. However, I guess I've lost another roommate."

Another major event that changed the life of Harmon Killebrew that fall was his marriage on October 1, 1955, to his high school sweetheart, Elaine Roberts. The couple was married at the Latter-Day Saints Mormon Church in Payette. Later they traveled to Cordoba, Mexico, 325 miles southeast of Mexico City, where Harmon played winter ball. He got to play regularly there, and he was beginning to sense some improvement in his play when tragedy struck the Killebrew family and he was called home to attend the funeral of his brother-in-law.

When Harmon reported to the Washington Senators in the spring of 1956, it was with the knowledge that this was a crisis year for him. The bonus clause had been amended and the two-year bench-warming provision discontinued. This meant he was eligible to be sent to the minors at any time the Washington brass decreed.

Naturally, Killebrew wanted to stay with the club, but he was realist enough to know that he had as yet done nothing to suggest that he might be retained by the Senators. There was, indeed, a very good chance that he would be shipped out for more seasoning.

"It's the sort of thing you have to expect in baseball," he told his wife, who had accompanied him to Florida. "It might be a matter of bouncing around a little at first, but in time I hope to make the Washington club and stay put."

"You'll make it, Harmon," said Elaine with wifely confidence. "I don't think it will be long either."

"You never know," said Harmon. "Anyway, if I'm farmed out I'll probably have a chance to play regularly, and that should help me."

Harmon was still with the Senators when they moved north, but when the season opened he was sitting on the bench. During April and May he got into only a few games —in a pinch-hitting role, mostly—and when June came around Harmon was certain the axe would fall.

It was early in June and the Senators had just completed a series with the Cleveland Indians at Cleveland's huge Municipal Stadium. Team members dressed quickly in the clubhouse, and the attendants took their bags as rapidly as possible and put them on a bus which was to take them to the airport. Harmon walked from the clubhouse and boarded the bus. At almost the same moment Howard Fox, traveling secretary for the Senators, caught up with him.

"I'm sorry, Harmon," he said. "You'll have to take your bags off the bus. I've just been informed they're sending you to Charlotte."

Harmon looked at Fox for a long time, letting the shock seep through him. He had been expecting something like this, but now that it had happened it seemed unreal.

"I've got a train ticket for you," Fox said, handing him an envelope. "The depot's just a few blocks from here. You've got an hour to make your train."

Harmon nodded and descended from the bus without a word. He saw Lavagetto and the manager frowned and said, "I'm sorry I couldn't give you more notice, Harm. But this could be a good thing for you. You'll get experience down there, and I wouldn't be surprised if you were back up here soon."

"Thanks, Cookie," said Harmon. "I'll do my best down there."

A soft rain started to fall as Harmon and the bus driver searched out his bag. Eddie Yost, star third sacker for the Senators, helped them look for it. The bag was finally found and Harmon shook hands with Yost and started to leave.

"Wait a minute, Harm," said Yost. "You'll get soaked to the skin. We'll get you a cab."

Harmon shook his head. "Thanks, Eddie," he said. "But I think I'd just as soon walk."

Harmon walked slowly toward the depot. Eddie Yost boarded the bus and looked out of the rain-splattered window at the retreating figure of the stocky young man from Idaho.

"That's about the saddest thing I ever saw, him walking away in the rain like that," he said to no one in particular. "He looks so doggoned forlorn."

"You know something," said Roy Sievers. "I'm betting the kid comes back."

4

~~~~~~

Charlotte, North Carolina, a town of approximately 100,000 people, boasted a Class A Atlantic League team called the Hornets. When Killebrew arrived he was greeted by the ex-American League catcher Rollie Hemsley, manager of the team.

"We can use an infielder," he said. "We'll play you at third, unless you're needed elsewhere. Is your wife going to join you down here?"

"Well, I guess not for a while anyway," said Harmon. "She's expecting a child soon, and she's back home in Payette."

"I see. Well, make yourself at home. The club attendant will suit you up. You'll get a chance to play down here, and that should help you."

"Yes, sir. I think it will help, all right."

As things turned out, Harmon did very well indeed at Charlotte. He played a reasonably steady third base, and he hit the ball with considerable authority. He stayed with the Hornets for 70 games, was at bat 249 times and gathered 81 hits for a neat .325 average. Included in his hits were 16 doubles, seven triples, and 15 home runs.

Naturally, this success made Harmon happy, but he was made even happier in August when he received word that his son had been born in a hospital at Ontario, Oregon, near Payette. The boy was named Cameron.

At almost the same time, Harmon got the news that some- one back with the Senators had taken note of his success with Charlotte and had recalled him. Harmon was excited at the prospect of returning to the Senators, and with some experi- ence behind him now, he felt sure he could do a better job for them if they would only give him a chance.

They did. Lavagetto put him in the lineup at various in- field positions and studied him closely. What he saw was a much improved ballplayer, but still an incomplete ballplayer who needed more work. At any rate, Killebrew appeared in 44 games with the Senators, but his hitting fell off. He batted only .222, slammed only 5 homers, and drove in a meager 13 runs.

Harmon Killebrew went back to Payette that fall with mixed feelings—delight at the opportunity of becoming bet- ter acquainted with his infant son, and dismay that he had not done better with the Senators.

That winter he had lengthy conversations with Elaine about his future in baseball. Whenever he began to doubt himself, she buoyed his confidence.

"I hit pretty good down in Charlotte," he said once, "but when I got back with the Senators I tapered off. There's a big difference between minor league and major league pitching, all right. In the minors you face a lot of pitchers who aren't too sharp. Their control is bad and they can't work the cor- ners. In the majors they can put the ball right where they want it, and they give you a real hitting problem up there."

"You've always been able to hit, Harmon," Elaine said. "And you'll hit in the majors too."

Spring training, 1957, was less than enchanting for Har- mon. The only really bright spot in the picture was the fact

that Elaine was with him in Florida. In a baseball sense, Killebrew did little to further his cause.

The previous year at Charlotte, Harmon had met another
young man who was equally determined to make the Washington team. His name was Bob Allison. During spring training at Tinker Field in Orlando, the two met again and, as
usual, discussed each other's chances.

"You have the best chance," said Allison. "After all, they
called you back last summer. They didn't call me."

"Yeah, but I didn't do very well," put in Harmon. "I only
hit two twenty-two, and I'm not the best glove man in the
world either."

"You think they'll keep either one of us this year?" asked
Allison, a dubious tone in his voice.

"Frankly, I think I'll be farmed out again. I just hope I
go to some team higher than Class A.

"Me, too," said Allison.

Before the spring training sessions ended, both players got
their wish. Both were sent down to Chattanooga to join the
Lookouts in the Class AA Southern League—one step up the
baseball ladder. Manager Cal Ermer greeted them with enthusiasm.

"Two big husky guys," he said. "They tell me you both
hit the long ball."

"Long, but not often enough, maybe," said Harmon modestly.

"Maybe down here you'll hit it both long and often," said
Ermer.

Killebrew was again installed in the infield and Allison
roamed the outfield. Almost immediately, Killebrew began
to click. In 142 games he batted .279, knocked in 101 runs,
and led the Southern Association with 29 home runs. Allison
was a little less successful, playing in 125 games and hitting
.246, batting in 38 runs and hitting only 2 homers.

Late in the season the Senators called back a group of minor leaguers for brief tryouts, and among them was Killebrew.

"Back you go again," said Allison, who had not been called. "I told you you had the best chance."

Harmon threw some clothing into a suitcase. "You'll get your turn," he said. "Maybe we'll both be up there next season."

The two had become warm friends, and they shook hands and wished each other success.

Harmon finished out the 1957 season by playing nine games for the Senators, so that his 9 hits in 31 times at bat for a .290 average, and his 2 home runs really didn't prove much, one way or the other.

Still, Harmon went home to Payette feeling much better after the 1957 season. He had had a good season with Chattanooga, and it had given him more confidence. Friends in Payette were sure that 1958 would find him a big leaguer, but Harmon was not one to boast or to make any predictions.

"You never know in baseball," was all he would say.

Harmon Killebrew reported to Orlando for spring training in 1958 with more confidence than he had ever enjoyed before. He felt strongly that his good year at Chattanooga had placed him in line for a shot at the Senator's third base job, even though veteran Eddie Yost would be a hard man to replace there. At the very worst, he felt sure he would be retained by the team as a substitute when Yost needed a rest or was injured. It seemed reasonable to assume that his minor league days were behind him and that from now on he would play in the heady atmosphere of the big leagues.

But Killebrew, who rarely got away to a fast start in spring training, was not overly impressive during the training period or in the Grapefruit League games. Lavagetto, watching him and comparing him with Yost, decided he had a problem on his hands. Killebrew seemed to have the most potential as a slugger, but Yost was the better glove man. And it was difficult to decide whether Harmon's power would make up for his defensive weaknesses, or whether Yost's talent with the glove would compensate for a lower batting average.

The issue was virtually decided one day when Harmon traveled to West Palm Beach with the Senators' B Team to play Kansas City's B outfit. The balance of the Washington club, including Yost, stayed in Orlando.

Late in the game with Kansas City, Harmon distinguished himself by hitting a long home run that tied the score and sent the game into extra innings. Then disaster struck. In the tenth inning Kansas City placed men on second and third with two out. The next hitter drove an easy hopper to Killebrew at third. Harmon set himself for the ball and fielded it easily. As he pulled back his arm to throw the hitter out at first, he saw Hal Smith, a slow Kansas City runner, coming from second to third. Then Rocky Bridges, the Senator shortstop, yelled, "Tag him! Tag him!"

Confused, Killebrew held up his throw, made a belated effort to tag Smith. Smith escaped the tag and slid into third base as the winning run went home.

In the clubhouse afterward, Killebrew sat in embarrassed silence. Finally Bridges approached him.

"I'm sorry, Harm. It was my fault. You were going to make the play at first, and that's where it should have been made."

"It's all right, Rocky. I should have ignored you and made the play. But I goofed it up."

Perhaps the incident would have been forgotten except for the fact that a sportswriter in Washington started his story of the game with: "Eddie Yost won the third base job for the Senators today, sitting in Orlando, Florida."

It was a brutal remark and seemed to be the final blow to

Harmon's hopes. He went north with the team, but when the Senators opened the American League season he had again found himself a well-polished place on the bench—and sat. Yost was the regular third baseman.

His friend, Bob Allison, was even less lucky. He was shunted off to the Chattanooga Lookouts again before the season opener.

"At least you're staying with the team," Allison told Harmon.

"Yeah. On the bench again."

Killebrew sat on the bench for almost a month, and during that time he was called on to pinch-hit twice. Then one day Cookie Lavagetto called him into his office.

"Harmon," he said. "I'm sorry, but I have to tell you that we're shipping you to Indianapolis."

Harmon felt the shock of the words cut through him. He shook his head.

"I thought maybe I could stick this year, Cookie," he said. "I had a good year with Chattanooga last season."

"I know you did, Harm. But Indianapolis is Triple A and we think the move will help you. Then, next year—"

Next year! It was always next year. Maybe, Harmon thought bitterly, I'm just another bonus baby who can't make good.

Killebrew was so upset by the news that he went to Ossie Bluege for advice. Ever since Bluege had signed him, he had served as a baseball father to Harmon, and it was a natural move for Killebrew to seek out the former Washington third baseman in a crisis.

"Ossie," he said. "I don't think I've got what it takes. I think I'd better quit baseball and go get a decent job somewhere."

"Don't talk like that!" snapped Bluege. "You've got plenty of potential. You're going to be a major leaguer, and a good

one. But it takes time, and things like going back to Triple
A just happen."

"I know," admitted Killebrew, "but there are a lot of com-
plications. My wife is expecting a second child any day now.
She's with me here in Washington, and if I go to Indianapolis, I'd like her down there with me—but I don't know if she
could make the trip so soon after having a child."

"It's easy to find out if she could," said Bluege. "Call the
doctor and ask."

"I suppose I could do that," said Harmon. "It's just that—
well, I thought I had a pretty good season with the Lookouts,
but maybe it wasn't as good as I thought because I didn't
get a chance to play up here, and now they're sending me off
to Indianapolis and—"

"Look, Harmon. Go to Indianapolis. Get your wife down
there when she can come. You'll play regularly and you'll
feel better. It's for your own good, Harm. Do it."

Finally, with some reluctance, Harmon decided to heed
Bluege's advice and go to Indianapolis. When he called the
doctor he was informed that in a reasonable time Elaine
would be able to join him.

So Killebrew joined the Indianapolis Indians in the Triple A American Association, reporting to manager Walker
Cooper. But from the first nothing went right for him. He
was despondent, worried about his wife, who had flown back
to Payette to have her baby, and concerned about his career.
Too many things fought for attention in Killebrew's mind,
and he was not able to concentrate on baseball as he would
have liked. Hits did not fall in for him with any degree of
consistency, and his fielding at third base left a lot to be
desired.

In May, Elaine bore another son and they named him
Kenneth. A short time later she wired that she was coming

to Indianapolis. The news gave Harmon a shot in the arm that he sorely needed.

On the day before Elaine was due to arrive in Indianapolis, Harmon rented an apartment and paid a month's rent in advance. But on that memorable day something else happened too. Harmon was notified that he was being sent back to Chattanooga!

It was the second hard blow for Harmon that year.

"How can I hope to make it in the majors," Harmon said, "when I can't even make it in Triple A?"

It was a question that nagged him. After all, he had played 38 games for Indianapolis, batted only .215, hit only 2 homers and knocked in a mere 10 runs. He also had made 11 errors for a fielding average of .907.

Elaine arrived the next day and together the couple drove to Chattanooga. One of the first persons to greet them was Bob Allison.

"I never expected you back here, Harm," he said.

"I didn't expect to be back," said Killebrew honestly. "But I'll tell you something. The chips are on the line for me now. If I don't do something down here—and right away—I'll never get another crack with the Senators."

"You and me both," said Allison.

Red Marion was now manager of the Lookouts, and he put Killebrew in the lineup immediately. In the first game Harmon smashed a line drive over the scoreboard 385 feet from home plate—the first player ever to clear the scoreboard with a drive.

"Maybe coming down here was good for you after all," Allison remarked, grinning. "It made you mad."

Harmon laughed. "I think I'll stay mad all season."

Killebrew did just about that. Although his fielding did not improve much, he picked up considerably in the hitting department. He played 86 games, banged out 17 home runs, drove in 54, and posted a batting average of .308.

And late in the season, when the last-place Washington Senators called a few minor leaguers back for a tryout, both Killebrew and Allison were among those summoned. In 13 games at the end of the season, Killebrew hit .194 for Washington, and in 11 games Allison hit .200. But those few games were not a genuine test for either player.

Killebrew and Allison both knew that spring training, 1959, would be the decisive one of their careers.

All through 1958 there had been talk about the Senators moving their franchise to some other town. For several years baseball had been in ferment. Conservatism had gone out the window, and in its place was a new daring. Club owners, who had maintained the status quo for years, saw one team after another leave for greener pastures. The Boston Braves had gone to Milwaukee, the St. Louis Browns had invaded Baltimore, and the Athletics had jumped to Kansas City. And when the New York Giants and Brooklyn Dodgers leaped clear to the West Coast, all the bars came down.

It seemed as if any team could move anywhere.

But Washington was different. Despite continued rumors that Cal Griffith was dickering with Minneapolis as a new site for the Senators, it did not seem possible for a team to desert the nation's capital. Fans and government officials alike felt that the Great American Game should have a franchise in Washington, and there were threats of legislation to stop any such move.

Even President Dwight D. Eisenhower pleaded for the club to stay in Washington. Still the rumors persisted. Minneapolis made a definite offer to the Senators. The twin city of St. Paul came in with a bid. Cal Griffith was asked point-blank

by reporters whether or not he intended to move the Senators out.

"We'll just have to wait and see," was his vague answer.

Then, abruptly, the rumors stopped—because the American League notified Griffith that it would not vote him
permission to move the franchise. That ended that, at least
temporarily.

With the club finally certain to stay in Washington at least
for the 1959 season, Griffith turned his mind to other matters
—namely, improving the club that had finished in the cellar
the season before.

One winter day Griffith made a deal that went a long way
toward settling Killebrew's fate. He traded third baseman
Eddie Yost to Detroit for infielder Reno Bertoia. Washington also parted with infielder Rocky Bridges and outfielder
Neil Chrisley, getting outfielder Jim Delsing and infielder
Ron Samford in return. But the two kingpins in the deal
were Yost and Bertoia.

"Bertoia is young and he can play second or third," said
Griffith.

"And if Bertoia makes it at second, who's on third?" Lavagetto wanted to know.

"Killebrew," said Griffith.

Lavagetto shook his head. "He's a nice guy, but he'll never
make it. He's a butcher in the field."

"He'll improve," said Griffith. "Give him a lot of work
down in Orlando next spring and see that he does improve.
Then play him at third. He'll cost you a few games with his
fielding, but I think he's got a chance to become a great
player. Let's give the kid his opportunity."

In the spring Killebrew arrived in Orlando knowing that
he faced a turning point in his struggle. With Yost traded
to the Tigers, third base was wide open for the taking. Bertoia
could take it, or any one of a half-dozen rookies coming up.

There would be heated competition for the job, no doubt about it, and Harmon knew that this time he could not afford to muff his opportunity. If he failed to make the grade, it would be all over for him.

Harmon was well aware that, despite Griffith's support, Lavagetto was giving him a *last look!*

Killebrew went to training camp determined to work hard —and he did. He took extra fielding practice until the sweat poured from his stocky body, and when the exhibition games started he fielded with at least ordinary skill. But to his chagrin, his hitting became lifeless! He was deep in a batting slump, and in the entire twenty-four-game exhibition schedule, Harmon did not hit one home run!

The slump worried Harmon. He knew that ability to hit the long ball was the one great asset he had, the one that would win him a permanent spot in the Senator lineup. If he failed in this, there would be no chance for him.

"What am I doing wrong?" he asked Lavagetto one day.

"You're lunging awkwardly at the ball," the manager said, "and you're hitting bad pitches. You better start studying the strike zone, Harm, or you're liable to end up right back in Chattanooga."

It was all too true. Harmon knew it. He was going for bad pitches and he was striking out a lot—on called third strikes. This meant he wasn't following the ball properly, wasn't really aware when the ball nipped the outside edge of the plate.

"When I'm in a slump," Harmon said to Allison, "every pitch is a borderline one. I swing at the bad ones and let the good ones go by for strikes. What's wrong?"

"You're trying too hard," said Allison.

Trying too hard? How could he be trying *too* hard? He couldn't let down, or he'd never make the grade. He had to stay in there, always swinging, always trying, never admitting that any pitcher had his number.

"Look, Harm! Don't worry about slumps," Ossie Bluege said one day. "I've had plenty myself. And there's no real solution. You just stand up there and keep swinging, and all at once they fall in for you and it's over. If anybody knew how to break a slump—really knew—they'd be worth a million dollars to this club or any other."

The veteran Jim Lemon befriended Harmon and also gave him good advice. "Study each pitcher, Harm," he said. "Knowing what each pitcher throws—and when he's liable to throw it—will get you out of a slump as quick as anything. Remember, every pitcher has a favorite pitch, and he's inclined to use it when he gets in a jam because he has confidence in it. This is a thing to remember; then you'll know what the pitcher is liable to throw when you come up in a clutch situation."

It goes without saying that Griffith, having virtually put his reputation on the line in trading Yost to give Killebrew a chance, lost a few pounds worrying about Harmon's lack of hitting during the Grapefruit League games. But he stuck with the young man.

"Play him, Cookie," he urged. "And if he doesn't make the grade, I'll take the rap."

On opening day, 1959, the Baltimore Orioles were the opposition and Vice President Richard Nixon, in a relief role for President Eisenhower, was in the Presidential box to throw out the first ball in opening ceremonies. The stands were filled with more than 25,000 fans.

The Senators had a lineup reputed to have a lot of power —or at least dormant power that, hopefully, might make itself felt. Bob Allison had made the team and was considered a good long-ball-hitting prospect, Jim Lemon was the cleanup batter with a penchant for slamming the ball out of the lot, and Killebrew, despite his lackluster spring record, was considered a potentially dangerous man. So was Roy Sievers, who was counted on to give the Senators a lot of support at the plate.

In addition, they had reasonably competent men such as Reno Bertoia at second, Ed Fitzgerald catching, Norm Zauchin at first and Ron Samford at short. For the opener, the crafty Pedro Ramos was given the honor of pitching.

When the pregame ceremonies were over and the national anthem played, the Washington Senators raced out to their positions on the field. A polite roar went up from the crowd, but not one that was overly enthusiastic because the Senators had finished last the previous two years. The crowd was content to sit back and wait, a long time if necessary, to see if this power-packed team really had improved.

Killebrew ran to his spot near the third base bag and nervously pounded his fist into his glove. The pressures of opening day were enough to give Harmon, not yet twenty-three years old, a whole nest full of butterflies in his stomach. But that was not all. This was the first year he had opened the season on the field, instead of on the bench. And the fact that he knew he was on a very hot spot, that this was his supreme test, and if he flunked it he would drift into baseball obscurity, made it even worse.

Ramos took his warm-up tosses in an easy, relaxed manner as Killebrew watched him with growing nervousness. Maybe, he thought, after the first batter or two he would relax, get into the swing of things.

At last the umpire signaled to play ball, dusted off the plate, and the Baltimore Orioles' first hitter, Willie Tasby, stepped into the batter's box. Killebrew crouched at his position, tense and waiting. Ramos shot a fast ball past Tasby for a strike. Then he hung a curve outside for ball one. The third pitch was in tight and Tasby swung.

The ball shot on the ground toward third base!

Killebrew moved to his right, got in front of the ball. He expected it to take the big hop into his hands, but it hugged the earth instead. Harmon went down with his glove, felt the ball smack against the heel of it and bounce away. Tasby legged it to first easily, and a low groan escaped the stands.

Killebrew felt the hairs on his scalp lift. He was so embarrassed he wanted to dash into the dugout and never come out again.

He had made an error on the very first play!

Fortunately the error did the Washington cause no damage, but Killebrew went back to the dugout after the inning shaking his head. Pedro Ramos came clattering down the steps and Harmon said, "A fine way for me to start the season. I'm sorry, Pedro."

"It's okay, kid," said the pitcher.

Harmon didn't hit on his first turn at bat, but in the fourth inning he faced Baltimore's Hoyt Wilhelm with Norm Zauchin on base. Wilhelm owned a fantastic knuckle ball that fluttered nervously about the plate, and when he could control it he was a mighty tough pitcher to hit. Killebrew was still somewhat an unknown quantity to American League pitchers, and Wilhelm tried him with a fast ball on the first pitch. But it stayed outside for a ball and Harmon ignored it.

The second pitch was a knuckler and Killebrew missed it. Then, with the count one-and-one, Wilhelm went back to the fast one again. Killebrew swung and the crack of the bat against ball was music in his ears. The ball rose in a majestic arc and landed in the stands for a home run!

As Harmon trotted around the bases he hung his head to hide a sheepish grin. At least he had made up for the error!

He felt suddenly much better than he had since the opening play of the game!

Washington went on to whip the Orioles 9–2 that day, and a happy bunch of players clattered into the clubhouse. Pedro Ramos sought out Killebrew at his locker.

"I guess you didn't have to apologize for that error," he said. "Thanks for the homer."

Both Killebrew and Bertoia were one-day heroes, for they had each hit one out of the park. And when Lavagetto dropped by to add his congratulations, Harmon began to feel that maybe, at long last, he really belonged.

5

Cookie Lavagetto kept Harmon in the lineup as the month of April progressed. During that time Killebrew collected a few hits, but he really didn't perform sensationally. By May 1 the Senators had a record of eight wins and nine losses and were dawdling about in fifth place. And Harmon was beginning to worry a little that perhaps Lavagetto might be contemplating some shuffling of the lineup—with disastrous results for himself.

But May turned out to be a charmed month for Harmon Killebrew, and it all started on the very first day of May.

The Senators were in Detroit for a series with the Tigers at Briggs Stadium. Jim Bunning, one of the stellar staff men of the Tigers, was on the mound to oppose them. Washington countered with Camilo Pascual.

It was a tight game all the way. Detroit got off to a running start by scoring two runs in the first inning. In the Washington half of the second, Killebrew came to bat with no one on base. When Bunning tried to get a fast ball past him, Killebrew drove it into the left field seats for his second homer of the season.

Pascual kept the Tigers under wraps long enough for the Senators to tie the score at 2-all in the top of the fourth, but

61

Detroit came back in the last of the sixth to go ahead 3–2. Then, just when things looked rather hopeless, Tiger errors by ex-Washington players Rocky Bridges and Eddie Yost permitted the Senators to tie it all up again at 3–3.

Neither team scored in the ninth and the game went into extra innings, with both starting pitchers still on the mound. In the top of the tenth Harmon found himself at bat with two out and no one on ahead of him. Bunning worked cagily on the husky Killebrew. Although Harmon had hardly yet established himself as a home run threat, still Bunning didn't like the size of his shoulders or the thickness of his arms.

Bunning delivered the first pitch, a curve that nipped the outside corner for a strike. The next pitch was in close for a ball. Bunning tested Killebrew with a screaming fast ball and Harmon swung and missed. With the count one ball and two strikes, Bunning tried to get Harmon to go for a bad pitch. But Harmon ignored two of them that broke outside and the count became three-and-two.

Killebrew stepped out of the box, got dirt on his hands, rubbed them on his pants leg, and stepped back in. He waved the bat menacingly for a moment, then cocked it over his right shoulder. Bunning came in with a pitch that broke away from the hitter, but Killebrew caught it on the fat of the bat. It rose like a skyrocket and slammed into the upper deck in left field for a tie-breaking homer.

It was his second home run of the game—the first two-home-run game of his major league career—and it held up as Pascual mowed down the Tigers in their half of the inning to preserve the 4–3 victory.

That, it seemed, was only the beginning.

On May 2 the Senators and Tigers clashed again, and in this one the Senators went wild. In the first inning Jim Lemon drew a walk and Killebrew hammered a tape-measure job into the upper deck in left field. In the fourth, with two on, Harmon repeated with another blow to the same spot. Roy Sievers got a homer and so did Ron Samford, and later Lemon poled one into the stands with the bases loaded. When the Senators were through shelling the hapless Tigers the score was 15–3. They had hit five home runs in nine innings for a club record, and had saddled the Tigers with their fifteenth loss in seventeen games.

And Killebrew's second two-homer game in two days gave the new Washington slugger five for the season.

The clubhouse was a bedlam after the game. It was a rare occasion when the Senators won a game so big, and they were in a shouting, happy frame of mind. Killebrew found himself shaking the hands of almost all his teammates as they congratulated him on his hitting. It was a very satisfying feeling to the young man from Idaho, but he was still embarrassed and shy about it all. When reporters crowded around for a statement, he couldn't think of anything to say except, "I just go up and try to hit the ball. If they go out, so much the better."

His modesty was put down to the fact that Harmon was still virtually a rookie, but what the reporters didn't know at that time was that Harmon would never change. No matter how heroic his acts, or how far he went in the game, he was never to lose his refreshing humility.

A few days later the Senators moved into Chicago for a go at the White Sox. Harmon continued his lusty hitting. He hammered Billy Pierce, ace of the Sox staff, for three hits— two singles and another home run, his sixth of the year. Lemon and Allison also hit round-trippers as Washington beat Chicago 8–3.

The following day Killebrew got only a single, while Allison hit a grand slam homer, and the Senators beat Chicago again, 6–4. Their western swing ended up as the most successful trip for the Senators in a decade. They had won seven and lost two.

By May 9 Killebrew was riding high. He was listed among the first five in runs batted in with nineteen, and he was leading the league in home runs with eight.

Washington moved into New York on that day, and aware of the Senators' recent winning ways, the Yankees started their ace, Bob Turley. Hal Griggs went to the mound for the Senators.

Harmon found that his bat was still red hot. With two out in the first inning and no one on, Turley decided to cool off the rampaging Killebrew. He brushed Harmon back with one pitch and finally worked the count to two-and-two. On the next toss Harmon sent the ball rocketing into the lower left field seats for his ninth home run of the season.

The show went on. In the fourth inning Killebrew sent a sharp single through the box and up the middle, but it did not figure in the scoring. By the time the eighth rolled around, Johnny Kucks was on the hill for the Yanks. He walked the leadoff batter, Bertoia, and Allison sent Reno heading for third with a single. With two ducks on the pond, Kucks went to his slider against Killebrew. It was low and away—and Harmon slammed it into the lower right field stands for his second home run and third hit of the day.

Washington won the game 9–0, with Griggs holding the Yanks to two hits. The surprising Senators were now in third place with fourteen wins and eleven losses. But the Yanks poured vinegar on the sweetness by beating the Senators twice on the following day, 6–3 and 3–2.

By now pitchers all over the league were beginning to realize they had a dangerous new hitter to face. In clubhouses all over the league there were discussions on how to stop the sudden and unexpected slugging of one Harmon Clayton Killebrew.

"What's his weakness?" was a frequently asked question. "I don't know. Maybe he doesn't have one."

"He hit one of my fast balls a mile," said one pitcher.

"He hit my best *curve*," said another.

"What makes him such a big hitter all of a sudden?"

This last was a reasonable question, and Killebrew himself was asked it by sportswriters covering the Senators' games. But young Harmon found it difficult to put his finger on anything that could account for his recent bombardment of American League hurlers.

"I'm not doing anything different," he said. "I'm just standing up there and swinging. I think it's just because I'm getting a chance to play all the time. It makes a lot of difference. When you're in and out of the lineup, you lose your timing. Playing regular, you get it back. That's the only answer I can give you."

There was little doubt, now, but that Lavagetto intended to play Killebrew regularly for some time to come. The manager had changed his tune about Harmon. "He always had potential as a hitter," he said. "It was his fielding I always worried about—and still do at times. But right now he's doing a lot for us with his hitting, and he isn't hurting us too bad in the field. This might be the year the kid really straightens out."

Another notable game occurred when the Detroit Tigers moved into Washington for a series. Frank Lary, ace of the Tiger staff, was on the pitching rubber for Detroit, and for five innings Lary had the Senators eating out of his hand. After five and a half frames Detroit was leading Washington, 3–0.

Then little Albie Pearson, leading off in the bottom half of the sixth, dented Lary for a single to right. Allison slammed a screaming double over first base and into right field, and by the time the Tiger right fielder, Al Kaline, ran it down,

Pearson had scored all the way from first. That brought up Killebrew.

Harmon stepped into the box and waggled his bat at Lary. Lary, an experienced pitcher, was well aware by this time of Killebrew's power, and he decided to brush the slugger back. A year ago it would not have occurred to any pitcher to brush Killebrew back with a tight pitch, but now he was suddenly a long-ball hitter and you had to intimidate him a little at the plate.

With Allison dancing off second, Lary went into his stretch, brought the ball down, glanced at Allison, and then whipped a high hard one inside. Killebrew saw the blur of white coming at him, spun around like a top and sprawled in the dirt. Lary got the ball back from his catcher and thought, *That ought to shake him up a little.*

Killebrew got up slowly. He brushed the dirt from his uniform, cleaned his hands on his shirt, looked at Lary a moment and stepped back into the box. He looked completely unruffled—and he was. Lary came in with a fast ball that was supposed to overpower a shaken Killebrew and Harmon swung. The ball soared on a line into left field and slammed into the seats 420 feet away to tie the score at 3–3.

"Whatsa matter, Lary?" roared a frog-voiced fan in the stands. "Won't the kid scare?"

The Tigers were not about to quit, however. In the top of the seventh, a single and a double put them out in front of the Senators by a 4–3 score. But the Washington team fought back to tie the score in the bottom of the seventh 4–4, and when Killebrew came to bat there were two men on the bases ahead of him. Lary had gone to the showers and reliefer Ray Narleski was pitching for the Tigers.

Narleski was a tricky pitcher with plenty of stuff, and he was determined not to give Killebrew anything good to hit. He worked a pitch outside, then in too close. Then he threw a strike, but low across the plate, hoping Killebrew would top it. Two balls and one strike.

Narleski tried for the outside corner on the next pitch and missed, sending the count to three-and-one. Killebrew stepped out of the box and got his signal—hit away.

Narleski tried to keep the ball on the outside so that Harmon wouldn't be able to pull it, but instead it slipped over the center of the plate. Harmon swung. The ball landed in the left field seats again for Killebrew's second home run of the game, putting the Senators ahead 7–4. That's the way the game ended.

After his sensational display of power, Killebrew tapered off for a few days. But on May 17 the Senators faced the Chicago White Sox in a doubleheader. Washington won the first game, 4–2, with Pedro Ramos pitching a five-hitter. Killebrew had a single and a double in four at bats. The second game was a wild twenty-eight-hit slugfest which Chicago won, 10–7. But Killebrew again hit two home runs—one off Bob Shaw and the other off Turk Lown.

At this point Killebrew's home run slugging came to a temporary halt, but in seventeen days from May 1 to May 17 he had accomplished a remarkable feat. He had had five two-homer games during that brief span!

And he was leading the league with a total of fourteen.

Killebrew, so long a bench warmer and a minor league bounce-about, had taken off like a skyrocket in the most amazing start in the memory of Senator fans.

6

~~~~~~

Followers of the Washington Senators had long been a patient lot, for the downtrodden team that represented the nation's capital was an almost perennial tail-ender. In the last four years they had finished last three times and in seventh place once. It was often said that "Washington is first in war, first in peace and last in the American League," and this cynical humor was substantially true.

But now, suddenly, something new and exciting had happened. From out of nowhere had come a chunky young lad with the ability to knock a baseball clear out of sight, and whether this astounding player could carry the Senators any higher in the standings didn't matter—the crowds came out to see Harmon Killebrew and his mighty swing.

Nor was Killebrew the only Senator to suddenly blossom out with unexpected power. There was substantial hitting from Bob Allison, Jim Lemon and Roy Sievers too, and these three along with Killebrew gave the Senators a "Murderer's Row" such as Washington had not seen in many years.

But Harmon Killebrew had established himself as the major attraction. Magazines and newspapers were flooded with stories about his prodigious home runs. When the team was home, Harmon found himself besieged with requests. The

Rotary Club and the Boy Scouts sought him as a guest speaker. Supermarkets wanted him to appear in their stores. Movie theaters demanded personal appearances, and manufacturers wanted him for their commercials. Sam Wong, an Oriental restaurant owner, even offered to give him a free Chinese dinner every time he hit a home run.

Killebrew was thoroughly amazed at all this. In fact, he was almost speechless. He found it difficult to answer the questions hurled at him by reporters who crowded around him after every game, much less speak to gatherings—which was entirely out of his line. He felt embarrassed and awkward about all the adulation coming his way, and didn't quite know how to cope with it.

Elaine had come to Washington that summer, and the couple had an apartment in Virginia. To his wife, Harmon poured out his thoughts.

"It's sort of frightening," he said. "People crowd around. Everybody wants me to attend banquets and meetings. I feel as if I should, too. After all, they're the fans and they pay my salary. Why shouldn't I try to appear when they want me?"

"But you can't go to all of them," Elaine objected. "You'll wear yourself out."

"I know. That's the bad part. I need all the rest I can get if I'm going to play ball well enough to stay with the club. And yet—"

It was a serious—and growing—problem. And Killebrew didn't know quite how to solve it. At last he was persuaded by club officials to change his telephone to an unlisted number, and he finally got some relaxation at home. But he found none at all at the ball park. He was dogged everywhere he went, exposed to the pressures of the press, the victim of an excited body of baseball fans who wanted to touch, and be near to, and get the autograph of, their current hero.

In these exciting days Killebrew learned when it was necessary to give of himself—and when to decline. He attended as many functions as his crowded schedule would permit, because he felt he owed it to his fans. Still he had no alternative but to turn down some engagements in the interest of keeping himself strong and alert enough to play his game. With reporters and photographers he cooperated endlessly, and between Harmon and the press there developed a close and friendly association. Sportswriters, in general, had only one complaint against the kid from Idaho—and it wasn't really a complaint at all.

"He's so modest," said one scribe, "that you can't get a thing out of him. He can hit two home runs in a day and when you ask him for a comment he just grins sort of sheepishly and says something about being lucky. That makes it tough to get a good quote out of him, but his humility is nevertheless refreshing."

On May 20 the Senators met the Cleveland Indians in Washington, and from the caliber of Killebrew's play that day the fans and sportswriters began to wonder if the pressure was beginning to affect him. Killebrew struck out three times that day, swinging wildly at several pitches, but he made up for it before the game was over by pumping a 430-foot home run two thirds of the way up in the left center field stands.

The Senators lost, 5–3, but Killebrew's fifteenth four-baser of the season gave him league leadership in homers and in runs batted in with thirty-two.

It was nine days later, on May 29, that Killebrew received one of the greatest thrills of his life. The Senators were taking batting practice before the game and Killebrew was standing near the cage watching his teammates take their swings. Lavagetto tapped him on the shoulder.

"There's a guy over in a box seat wants to see you," he said.

Killebrew looked around. "Yeah? Who?"

"President Eisenhower," said Lavagetto calmly.

Harmon almost choked. "You're kidding!"

"No. He's in the Presidential box. He wants to meet you."

Killebrew glanced over at the Presidential box, and sure enough, President Eisenhower was sitting there with several government officials. Harmon walked toward the President's box with his heart thumping wildly. Imagine him meeting the great man who had led Allied forces against the Germans in World War II and who had subsequently become President of the United States! It was all he could do to force his legs to carry him in the right direction.

As Killebrew approached the stands, President Eisenhower smiled his broad smile and extended his hand. Killebrew shook it solemnly.

"I'm very glad to meet you, Mr. President," he said.

"I'm glad to meet you," said Eisenhower. "My grandson, David, is a great fan of yours."

"Thank you very much, Mr. President," Killebrew answered. "I—I wonder if you'd do me a favor. Would you autograph a ball for me?"

The President beamed. "Of course," he said, "but only on one condition—that you autograph one for my grandson."

Two balls were quickly supplied, and Killebrew and the President of the United States exchanged autographs. That afternoon Killebrew hit his seventeenth home run of the season and two singles in four times up to lead the Washington Senators to a 7–6 win over Boston. Then he went home and placed the ball autographed by President Eisenhower in a special place of honor.

"Not many people get the President's signature," he said to Elaine. "I'm real proud of that."

Despite the fact that Killebrew, Sievers, Allison and Lemon were all bombarding the fences for Washington, the Senators remained generally ineffective. They were a peculiar team in

1959. They had as much power as any outfit in the league, and they were a nightmare to every pitcher who faced them. But, unfortunately, they had nothing else. Their pitching sparkled in spots but was mostly average, and their fielding had become almost ludicrous. As a result, the Senators languished deep in the second division through most of the 1959 season, and the heroics of their home run hitters weren't enough to pull them up any higher.

By June 1 the Senators were in seventh place with twenty-one wins and twenty-six losses, and Cookie Lavagetto knew better than anyone that there was little prospect of doing any better.

Through the month of June, Killebrew, batting around .272, continued to make the walls and fences of American League parks a target. On June 12 he blasted a home run against the Cleveland Indians at Griffith Stadium that was to have historic importance—after the season ended. It was the first inning and Cleveland's top pitching star, Herb Score, was on the mound. With two out and no one on, Killebrew straightened out one of Score's slants and lined it into the left field stands. But before half the game was completed, a deluge of rain washed out the ball game and the home run did not count—a fact that had considerable importance when the final home run figures for the season were all in.

Killebrew, never one to worry over a lost home run, hit one the next day and continued his barrage at a steady pace. But Harmon had his bad days too. In mid-June, Vice President Richard M. Nixon came out to the ball park to watch the player all Washington was excited about. The Senators beat the Tigers twice that day, 4–3 and 7–5, but Killebrew was of little help. He hit one single in eight times at bat.

But for the most part, Harmon's hitting barrage continued unabated. And the Senators, profiting by it, clawed their way up to sixth place by midseason.

Killebrew, by this time, had acquired a new nickname. Reporters called him "Killer," and the fans picked the name up at once. And so great were Harmon's exploits in the first half of the 1959 season that the "Killer" found himself chosen on the American League All-Star team, a fact that pleased and thrilled him.

"It's a real honor," he said to Elaine. "I remember how I sat down there in a Chattanooga hotel room and watched the All-Star Game last year on television. I guess I was feeling pretty low at the time, because I figured I never was going to make it. Now, the very next year, I'm in it. It's hard to believe."

"How could they keep you off, the way you've been pounding the ball," said Elaine stoutly.

The All-Star Game was played in Pittsburgh that year and the National League won a squeaker, 5–4. Killebrew did not distinguish himself, going oh-for-three, but the very fact that he was included in a game that had all the stellar members of both leagues on display gave him one of the big thrills of his career.

Although Killebrew's hitting was the sensation of the baseball world, his fielding was nothing to boast about. He was having a rough season at third base, but for the first time in his career his contribution in the RBI department was more than making up for fielding inadequacies. But Harmon was serious and determined to improve himself, and on many occasions he came to the ball park early to work on his fielding.

Lavagetto's appraisal of the Killer had changed again. "He's a gutty kid, and he's going to be one of the greats of the game," he said one day. "He'll get to be a better glove man because he'll work at it. As for his hitting, how can you keep him out of the lineup?"

When a batter hits home runs with the frequency that Killebrew hit them in 1959, it's inevitable that sportswriters will begin to compare him with the immortal Babe Ruth. Harmon's experience in this regard was the same as others before and since. Calculations on whether or not Harmon could beat Babe Ruth's record of sixty home runs in a season began to appear in newspapers. The mild-mannered Killebrew almost blushed when he read them.

"Imagine," he said, "comparing me with Ruth! This is my first good year and Ruth had dozens of them. It's silly!"

But on July 11 Killebrew supplied more ammunition for the sportswriters' guns. In a game with the Baltimore Orioles at Griffith Stadium, Killebrew hit a first-inning home run off Hal Brown that carried 450 feet. It was his thirtieth homer of the season, and that's what ticked off the speculation. Killebrew had now joined a long list of sluggers who, at one point in their careers, had been ahead of Babe Ruth's famous 1927 pace. Ruth had hit his thirtieth four-baser in his eighty-third game. Killebrew had hit his thirtieth homer in his eighty-second game.

The speculation finally inspired Washington sports columnist Shirley Povich to write a studious article evaluating Killebrew's worth to the Washington Senators. It said:

"It is not necessary to measure Killebrew in terms of a threat to Babe Ruth's record of sixty. If he fails that goal, he will still be a considerable personality. This lad has been an exciting ballplayer. He doesn't have to break Ruth's record or come very close to give Washington fans a remarkable show. He has done that already. Those muscles have been exciting. He doesn't have to hit the ball on the nose to get a home run. Just a piece of it is often sufficient. It may be said simply that Harmon gives Washington fans a lot to look forward to."

Nevertheless the speculation continued, for by July 16

Killebrew had actually gained on Ruth's record. On that date Harmon hit a Jim Bunning pitch into the left center field stands to lead the Senators to a 3–0 victory over the Tigers. It was his thirty-first homer in his eighty-fifth game. The newspapers were quick to point out that the legendary Ruth had not hit his thirty-first homer until his ninety-fourth game.

"Killebrew is nine games ahead of Ruth's record!" screamed the papers.

But he was not to beat Ruth's record. In August and September Killebrew's home run production tailed off. He hit only fourteen after the All-Star Game, and as Killebrew went, so went the Senators. In one horrendous stretch between July 20 and August 10 the hapless Senators lost eighteen straight games! That was enough to deposit them in the American League cellar for keeps!

Of course, speculation went in another direction then. Why had Killebrew tailed off in the last two months? What was wrong? When president Cal Griffith was asked to explain the phenomenon, he had a ready retort.

"Look!" he snapped. "This kid has been under pressure all year long. He's been followed everywhere he's gone. Killebrew is conscientious; he tries to cooperate with everyone and gives of his time freely. When people ask him to make personal appearances, he tries to comply. He doesn't want to let anyone down. And don't forget, you guys wrote a lot of stuff about how great he was, and naturally Harmon read it, and then he began to think that he had a big reputation to live up to and he began to press, and the more he pressed the less he accomplished. And that's what happened."

Griffith was right. Killebrew would have been less than human if he had not felt the tremendous pressure of being a home run hero. With no previous record to hint at it, he had become the American League's top slugger—and the sudden adulation was too much to take. He began to press at the plate and his hitting fell off.

Despite his second-half slump, however, Killebrew headed into the last days of September trailing Cleveland's Rocky Colavito for the home run title by only one round-tripper. On September 23, a week before the end of the season, Colavito had forty-one and Killebrew had forty.

"You think you can beat the Rock?" was the natural question.

"I don't know," said Harmon. "I'll just keep swinging."

Both Colavito and Killebrew picked up another homer that week, and when the last game of the season rolled around the home run score was Colavito forty-two, Killebrew forty-one.

On the final day of the year Washington lost to the Boston Red Sox, 6–2. But Killebrew received one of the big thrills of his life when, in the fifth inning with bases empty, he hit a towering homer off Jerry Casale that tied Colavito for the home run championship at forty-two each! Later Harmon was to say that it was one of the most memorable homers of his career.

Despite the slugging of Killebrew, Allison, Sievers and Lemon, the Senators posted an incredibly poor record for 1959. The team's batting average ended up at .237, lowest in the league, and they were seventh in fielding. They finished twenty-one games behind the Chicago White Sox, who captured the pennant, and seven games behind the Kansas City Athletics, who ended in seventh place.

But Killebrew's personal statistics for 1959 were almost unbelievable. His slump during the second half of the season had pulled down his batting average to .242, but in other respects he led the Senators in a variety of hitting achievements. He led the club in home runs with 42, in doubles with 20, in runs scored with 98, in total bases with 282, in walks with 90, and in slugging percentage with .516. He also drove in 105 runs. On the dark side of the picture, however, was the fact that he led the league in errors with 30.

But overall it was a fine season, and Harmon was later honored by the Idaho State Society for his accomplishments. Only one ironic sidelight intruded. Had the home run that Harmon hit on June 12, when the game was rained out before it became a regulation contest, counted, he would have passed Colavito and won the home run championship outright!

7

President Calvin Griffith had not given up in his efforts to move the Senators out of Washington, but he was having difficulties getting the necessary backing from other club owners. It was still the opinion of the league that the nation's capital should not be without a baseball team, and this as much as anything worked against a transfer.

Meantime, Killebrew's fantastic 1959 season had created a great amount of interest among owners of other clubs. This interest reached a peak one day when Gabe Paul, then general manager of the Cincinnati Reds, called Griffith on the phone.

"I'm interested in Killebrew," he said bluntly.

"Who isn't?" retorted Griffith.

"I'm prepared to offer a lot of money for him," said Paul persuasively. "I'll give you half a million dollars for his contract."

It was a tremendous amount, and if any club could use that kind of money it was the downtrodden Washington Senators. But Griffith turned it down. Later he told newspaper reporters, "You can't play half a million bucks at third base. I'm hanging on to Harmon."

It was a high compliment to Harmon, and it wasn't lost on him. When Killebrew heard about the offer he let out a low whistle. "It kind of shakes me that somebody would offer that much money for my contract," he said. "But it shakes me even more to think that Mr. Griffith turned it down."

During the winter of 1959–60, Killebrew kept himself busy by taking a sales job with the Inter-Mountain Gas Company in Payette, Idaho. He had to have something to keep his mind occupied, for he was concerned about the upcoming 1960 season. He figured he would have to put together another big season to repay Griffith for his confidence. And when Griffith signed him before the 1960 season for $20,000, he was sure of it.

Cookie Lavagetto was again signed to manage the stumbling Senators in 1960—a vote of confidence from the front office. But Griffith was determined to improve the player personnel, and one important addition he wanted to make to the team was a hitting catcher. Finally, two weeks before the season opened, Washington obtained Earl Battey from the Chicago White Sox in exchange for first baseman–outfielder Roy Sievers. It was a calculated gamble to give up a portion of their power, but they felt that Battey would take up at least some of the slack at the plate and would do a better job of handling the Senator pitching staff.

Killebrew reported to Orlando wanting badly to have a good spring training, but it turned out to be only average. He spent a great amount of his time trying to improve his fielding. Under the torrid Florida sun he sweated off pound after pound as he stabbed at grounders hit to his left and right, or scooped up sizzling grass-cutters hit directly at him. One of the toughest plays for him to make—and this has always been a tough one for third basemen—was to come in on a topped pitch down the line and throw the runner out at first.

"You have to move in fast, have sure hands and throw while you're running and bent over," said Lavagetto. "It isn't easy, but it's one of the plays a third baseman has to be able to make."

"Who in the league makes that play well?" snorted Ossie Bluege, who was sensitive to any criticism of his protégé. "Nobody—that's who!"

But Killebrew was drilled on it, and he got better as spring training advanced. By the time the team moved north for their opening game, his fielding had improved to the point where Lavagetto was confident that Harmon could hold down the third base job without serious consequences to the team.

Again in 1960, the Senators offered a power-packed lineup. The three top sluggers were Killebrew at third base, Allison in right field and Lemon in left field. Added to this hard-hitting trio were such players as Billy Gardner at second, Len Green in center, Don Mincher at first, and Earl Battey catching.

As the season opened, for the first time Harmon felt a comfortable sense of security at his position. There was no reason to think that he wouldn't be able to pound the ball with the same authority in 1960 as he had in 1959. And his fielding had improved to the point where he felt that this year he could avoid leading the league in errors.

But it is often at these times that things begin to fall apart—and they did for Killebrew. In 1959 he had started off with a loud bang and tapered off to a whisper at the end of the season. In 1960 the situation reversed itself. Harmon got away to a slow, stodgy start. Nothing he hit seemed to fall safe for him, and the home run power in his bat was dormant.

Then, to complicate matters, he pulled a hamstring muscle, the large tendon at the back of the knee, and the injury put him on the bench for a month. When he left the lineup he was hitting .256 and had collected only four home runs.

Killebrew sat gloomily on the bench, nursing his painful injury, agonizing at his inability to play. For a home run

slugger who had belted forty-two round-trippers the year before, sitting on the bench until midseason with only four in
the bag was an aggravating situation. Besides, Reno Bertoia,
who had replaced him at third base, was going good—and
Harmon began to wonder if he would ever get back in the
lineup again. Finally, on the fourth of July, Lavagetto put
the eager Killebrew back in the game against Cleveland—but
not at third base. Instead, he was installed at first base.

It was a dreadful day. Harmon found that his long sojourn
on the bench had hurt his timing. He swung late on fast
pitches and early on slow ones. He made the mistake of going for bad balls. In a long afternoon for Washington, in
which Cleveland beat the Senators twice, Killebrew managed
to get only one soft blooper single in eight times up. When
the count reached two singles in nineteen trips to the plate,
Lavagetto benched him again.

The benching lasted only one day, for on the following day
the manager put Harmon back in the game. His season's batting average, at that moment, was .233.

"You're worrying about your hitting," Lavagetto told Harmon before the game. "Don't try to change anything you're
doing up there. You have a good swing, just keep using it.
The hits will come."

Each time Killebrew went to the plate that day, he talked
to himself. *Relax,* he'd say, *take it easy, stay loose.* He was
making a deliberate, conscientious attempt not to press.

The results were surprising. In the fifth inning, with Baltimore leading, 2–0, Killebrew clobbered one into the left field
bleachers with the bases empty to close the gap to 2–1. In the
sixth inning the Senators tied the score, and in the eighth
they rallied for five runs, Harmon's contribution being his
second home run of the game. When it was all over, Killebrew had added a single to his day's work to make it three-for-
four, and Washington had won the game, 7–2.

The two-homer game was the first big game of the 1960 season for Killebrew, and it had come in the last half of the season. They were only his fifth and sixth homers of the year, not an impressive mark for a young man whose entire future depended on knocking baseballs out of major league ball parks.

Despite Killebrew's personal woes, however, the Washington club was doing well—for them. They had won eleven out of their last sixteen games and were in sixth place. Jim Lemon was carrying the bulk of the hitting burden, and by July 10 he had twenty home runs and was selected for the American League All-Star team.

Killebrew was delighted at Lemon's good fortune. Lemon, now thirty-two years old and nearing the end of his playing days, had for two years given advice to the twenty-four-year-old Harmon. The two had become almost inseparable. They always sat together on airplanes as they flew from one city to another, and they had long discussions on every phase of the game. Killebrew found Lemon's baseball wisdom a godsend.

"I'm glad you made the All-Star Game," said Harmon sincerely. "You deserve it. I'm not surprised that I didn't. I've been doing badly all year. I guess all I can do is keep plugging away."

"Harmon, you're the most conscientious guy I ever met," said Lemon. "That's what you've got in your favor. You'll never quit no matter how tough things get. You'll overcome your problems. We all have slumps and bad years. This might be one of yours, but more likely you'll straighten out and end in a blaze of glory. Just keep trying, that's all it takes."

The first All-Star contest of the year was played at Municipal Stadium in Kansas City and the Nationals won, 5–3. Two days later the second All-Star game was played at Yankee Stadium in New York, and again the Nationals won, 6–0.

When the regular season resumed, the pace of Killebrew's

hitting stepped up a bit, just as Lemon had predicted. And with his hitting improved, Killebrew found that he also felt more comfortable playing first base. He had felt strange and out of place at the position for some time, but now he was becoming accustomed to it. Ground balls hit to first were not much different from those hit to third, and he was catching on to the problem of shifting his feet as he took the throws of the infielders.

But baseball is an uncertain business, and it was extremely uncertain for Killebrew in 1960. Just about the time he was mastering first base play, Lavagetto put Harmon back at third. Julio Becquer, a newly acquired Cuban ballplayer, was placed at the initial sack.

Killebrew took the move in stride. He kept right on hitting, and on August 2 had another two-homer game against Cleveland. In the clubhouse Allison shook his hand.

"You're on the beam again," he commented.

"It's about time," said Harmon. "But maybe it's too late for me to have much of a record this year."

"You're not the only one in trouble. I have only half as many homers this year as last. What did they do, anyway— deaden the ball?"

"Maybe the pitchers are just getting wise to us," said Harmon with a grin.

"I'd hate to think so," said Allison.

Killebrew's first half performance had not diminished the affection the Washington fans had for him. They recognized that he had been hurt for much of the first half of the season, and that it would take time for him to get back in the hitting groove again—and now that he appeared to be back, there were the usual cheers, the usual demand for personal appearances, the usual crush for autographs.

Killebrew, always sincere, recognized these requests as part of the job. He was flattered that so many people wanted to

see him and talk to him, and he tried to fulfill all of his obli-
gations. But he was modest and unassuming by nature, and
he much preferred to be alone or in a small company of close
friends. And he treasured his home life, and the chance to be
with Elaine and the two children, Cameron and Kenneth.
Elaine lived with the children in Washington during the season, and Harmon spent every moment of his free time with
them. When he was on the road, the pressure slackened some.
He spent much of his time reading in his hotel room, watching TV or attending movies. Often the other players would
try to lure him into playing cards, but he did not enjoy cards.

"I think I'll go to my room and watch TV," he would say.

"Big deal," somebody would comment. "Have an exciting
evening."

"I will," Harmon would promise with a grin.

Harmon continued his assault on American League pitchers. One day in Kansas City the A's started their ace pitcher,
Ray Herbert, against Washington. The Senators greeted him
with extreme rudeness. In the first inning Len Green and
Reno Bertoia both singled and Killebrew walked up to the
plate. Herbert looked in for the sign, nodded his head, and
delivered a ball in close to Harmon's chest. The next pitch
slipped over the corner for a strike. One-and-one.

The Kansas City fans were silent. They knew the power of
Killebrew, and they waited with strained patience to see how
Herbert would cope with him.

The crafty Herbert teased Killebrew with a slider, and the
umpire's voice cut the quiet.

"Stee-rike!"

With the count one-and-two, Herbert wasted one and the
count was even. Killebrew stepped out of the box, knocked
dirt from his spikes, and stepped back in. He waved his bat
twice, then cocked it high over his right shoulder.

The pitch came in, a sizzling fast ball, higher than Herbert wanted it. Killebrew swung. The ball rose like a skyrocket and fell into the left field stands for a three-run homer!

It was Killebrew's sixteenth of the season.

Kansas City picked up a run in the first inning to make the score 3–1, but in the third Washington got going again. Killebrew opened with a sharp single to center. Faye Throneberry dropped one into left field, and Killebrew stopped at second. He came racing home with the fourth Washington run when Jose Valdivielso smashed one on the ground over second.

Kansas City kept picking away at the Senators' 4–1 lead, and when the seventh opened the score was 4–3. Herbert was still pitching when Killebrew came up with nobody on ahead of him. Herbert decided to stay away from high fast balls, feeding him low curves instead. But Killebrew caught one on the fat of the bat and drove the ball high into the stands for his seventeenth home run of the year, making the score 5–3. Since the Athletics picked up one in the ninth, the run proved to be the winning margin. Killebrew had accounted for all five of Washington's runs in the 5–4 victory.

By August 14, mainly on the strength of Killebrew's sensational hitting, the Senators were amazing the entire league. They were in fourth place!

Besides hitting homers, Killebrew was gradually boosting his batting average by getting two or three hits a day. In August he hit thirteen home runs to pace the club and by the end of that month he had twenty-three.

About this time another unforgettable event took place in Killebrew's life. Harmon had always been interested in national politics, and 1960 was the year that Senator John F. Kennedy and Vice President Richard M. Nixon were hotly campaigning for the Presidency. Nixon's campaign manager thought it a good idea for Nixon to associate with prominent athletes, and he invited a number of players, including Killebrew, to become members of what he called the "Dick Nixon

Sports Committee." Nixon was then billed as sports' "No. 1 Fan."

During the early days of the Presidential campaign, Nixon injured his left knee and was taken to Walter Reed General Hospital in Washington to undergo treatment for an infection. It was a blow to Nixon's campaign plans as he fretted away time in the hospital.

One day Killebrew was asked if he would visit the Vice President, along with other athletes.

"It would be an honor," said Killebrew.

On August 29 a group of prominent athletes visited the Vice President at the Capitol. Among them were Killebrew and Jim Lemon of the Washington Senators; Roy Sievers, now of the White Sox; Frank Gifford, halfback for the New York Giants pro football team; Florence Chadwick, the swimmer; and Wiffi Smith and Marilyn Smith, professional golfers.

Killebrew opened the month of September by hitting three home runs in the first five days. Then on September 11 the Senators met the Tigers at Briggs Stadium in a doubleheader. Detroit won the first game easily, although Killebrew hit a bases-empty homer off the Tigers' star hurler, Frank Lary. In the second game the Tigers won 8–5, but it wasn't Harmon's fault. Killebrew drove in all of Washington's runs with two homers, his twenty-eighth and twenty-ninth of the season. The first one came in the second inning with two runners aboard and the second in the eighth with one man on. Both were hit off Bill Fischer. One of the blasts struck the facing of the roof in left field—and stadium observers said they could not remember a longer home run in that section.

"It *was* a pretty good one," Killebrew admitted in the clubhouse as reporters surged around him. "And three in one day is always a big power day."

The Washington Senators surprised the league by finishing fifth in 1960, ahead of Detroit, Boston and Kansas City. Killebrew settled for 31 home runs compared to 42 the season before, but he had missed almost two months' play. He batted .276, better than the year before, and drove in 80 runs. And even more significant, his fielding improved; he made only 17 errors for a .978 average.

8

~~~~~~

October 26, 1960, was a red-letter day in the history of the Washington Senators. That was the day officials of the American League clubs held a high-level meeting at the Savoy-Hilton Hotel in New York and voted to expand the league to ten teams.

This was the open sesame for which the Senators had been waiting. At the same meeting they were granted permission to move their franchise from Washington to the twin cities of Minneapolis and St. Paul in Minnesota. Still, the American League owners were reluctant to leave the nation's capital without a big league ball team, and voted to bring a new team into Washington. They also opened the door to a new team representing Los Angeles.

Up in Minnesota there had been a running battle for some time between the Chambers of Commerce at Minneapolis and St. Paul. The two cities, on opposite sides of the Mississippi River, had long been rivals. Both wanted a big league team to play in their city, and both had for some time been advocating sites for the new ball park. But at last the conflict was settled by mutual agreement—the ball park would be built in suburban Bloomington, south of the twin cities and about equidistant from the two. So that neither city would gain an upper hand in association with the ball club, the team was called the Minnesota Twins—the first major league ball club to be named after a state instead of a city!

At home in Payette, Harmon heard about the move and welcomed it. He had liked playing in Washington, but he was also fond of the more open country around the Minneapolis–St. Paul area.

"You have to see those cities to appreciate them," he told Elaine. "When I was with Indianapolis in the American Association, we used to go up there, and I always enjoyed it. It's nice fresh country, the kind we have out here."

Elaine looked fondly at their two children. Kenneth was now two and a half years old and Cameron was past four.

"Cameron will be old enough for school soon," said Elaine. "Maybe by that time we could move permanently to Minneapolis."

Harmon nodded. "We'll see how things go. Baseball's never a certain thing."

"It's pretty certain they're not going to trade *you*," said Elaine with a trace of pride in her voice.

Killebrew spent his winter in snow-bound Payette, working again for the Inter-Mountain Gas Company, and he kept in shape by hunting, fishing and visiting the high school gym for workouts. He was now quite a celebrity around town, and people liked to stop him on the street and talk to him—often people who said they knew him when he was "just a little bit of a kid." He was considerably more than that now. He had reached the age of twenty-four and had attained his maximum height and weight. He was five feet eleven inches tall, but looked somewhat shorter because of his square, rocklike build. His body was large, with a thirty-five waist. He wore a forty-four jacket. But his legs were short, giving him a squatty look. He had a thick neck, wide shoulders and a set of arms made for professional wrestling—or for hitting home runs.

Harmon Killebrew was a compact package of power.

But what endeared Harmon to most of his neighbors was his sincerity. His success as a big league ballplayer had left him unspoiled. He was modest and unassuming about his accomplishments and inclined always to belittle them rather than build them up. One writer expressed his opinion of Killebrew this way:

"Everything about him suggests the characteristics of the humble apple of the earth, the state fruit of Idaho. Modest, unassuming, self-effacing, mild-mannered, folksy—all of those."

But Harmon was restless, as he always was, to get going on the 1961 season. When he received his contract through the mail, he was delighted to see that it contained a $7,000 raise, despite the fact that he had been out a month and had hit eleven fewer homers as a result. It made him all the more eager to prove his worth to the team that would now be the Minnesota Twins.

There was only one uncertainty in Harmon's mind when he reported to Tinker Field in Orlando for the 1961 spring training season—and it was a big one. He didn't know where he was going to play. He had started the 1960 season at third base and had jumped between that position and first base throughout the year. Actually, he liked first base better now, but his preference was not what would decide the issue. The matter would be decided by Lavagetto, with the good of the team in mind.

"Bring a first baseman's mitt and a third baseman's glove," Lavagetto had told him. "You ought to end up at one of those places."

Killebrew was tried out at both. He had considerable competition for the third base spot, for Reno Bertoia was battling for a place on the team and so was a young man named Billy Gardner. When the Grapefruit League games got under way,

Harmon played at both positions, which gave him little opportunity to excel at either one. However, his batting was not affected by the fielding changes. He enjoyed one of his best spring training sessions by hitting six home runs.

His consistency with the bat was a matter of great concern to most of the sportswriters visiting the camps. Much to Harmon's surprise, a lot of them still seemed to think he had a chance to beat Babe Ruth's 1927 record of sixty home runs, and he was asked endlessly whether or not he thought he could do it. In his self-effacing way, he tried to answer each question with patience. A typical interview occurred one day when Tom Briere, sportswriter for the *Minneapolis Tribune*, caught him in an idle moment.

"Harmon," he said, "you've had fifteen hits this spring and six of them have been homers. That must be the best spring training you ever had, isn't it?"

"I guess it must be," said Killebrew. "At least, I don't remember ever hitting six homers before in spring exhibition games."

"I suppose you've been asked this before," said Briere, "but I'm going to ask it again. Does this mean you'll break Ruth's home run record?"

"I really haven't given it much thought."

"You must have been asked about it," said Briere.

"Oh, sure. But I've just never been too concerned about it."

"Why not?"

"Well, I just try to hit the ball. Right now I'm trying to hit up through the middle and get my timing back."

"Isn't your aim this season sixty home runs?"

"No. I can't say that. Sure, I'd like to hit sixty. But you know, I struck out more than a hundred times last year, and my real desire this season is to cut down on my strikeouts."

Briere decided to change the subject. "Do you know if you'll play at first or third yet?" he asked.

Harmon shook his head. "I like it at first because I feel more relaxed there. But I'll play where Lavagetto wants me to play."

"Where do you think the Twins will finish?"

"It's hard to say," hedged Harmon. "I see one guy picked us for seventh. But I think we'll make the first division."

Shortly before the season started Lavagetto pulled a surprise. He made Killebrew team captain.

"He's a great kid but a little quiet," explained Lavagetto. "This will put him on the spot and make him into a take-charge guy. He'll be the one to talk to pitchers during a crisis, and he'll have the authority to argue with umpires on questionable calls."

"It's an honor and I appreciate it," said Harmon about the promotion. "I guess I don't talk much, but I think a man can set an example for his team by his actions on the field."

As the team moved north for its opener, speculation about the possibility of Ruth's record being broken persisted, much to Killebrew's dismay. Once a reporter asked Lavagetto whether he thought either Killebrew or Jim Lemon had a chance.

"Killebrew, if anybody," said the manager quickly. "After all, he's only twenty-four and he's improving. He hasn't yet reached his full potential."

That brought the question right back to Harmon again and he remained noncommittal. "It's too hard to predict such a thing," he said logically. "You have to be awfully lucky to hit sixty. I'm just trying to play one game at a time, cut down on my strikeouts and increase my average. I'm not really worried about home runs."

Although a lot of newspaper sportswriters didn't seem to understand this, it was true that Harmon was less enthusiastic about home runs than his followers. He knew he had the strength to propel the ball out of the park if he got a good piece of it, but his main concern was merely to get a hit when he strode to the plate. The home runs, he felt, would come as a matter of course.

The newly formed Minnesota Twins opened their first major league season in New York against the Yankees. Just before the game Lavagetto made a statement to the press.

"We're going to surprise a lot of people this season," he said. "We're a better club than a lot of people give us credit for. We're going to make it tough for a lot of teams."

The baseball experts who try to evaluate the teams before the season were picking Minnesota to finish anywhere from fourth to sixth. Most baseball men agreed that the Twins had power to spare. But their fielding was questionable and their pitching spotty. Still, the lineup looked fairly impressive. Leadoff hitter for the Twins was Zoilo Versalles, the shortstop. Trailing him in the batting order were Len Green, center field; Harmon Killebrew, who had finally ended up on first base; Jim Lemon in left; Bob Allison in right; Earl Battey behind the bat; Reno Bertoia at third; Billy Gardner at second; and for the opener, Pedro Ramos pitching.

To the Yankees it must have looked like a formidable lineup, for Allison and Bertoia both slammed homers to pace the Twins to an opening day victory, 6–0. Killebrew hit a single and drove in Versalles with a run on a sacrifice fly.

The next day it rained and the Twins moved on to Baltimore. Minnesota was bombed 8–0 by the Orioles, but that was only half of the sad story.

It was the ninth inning and the Orioles had already tucked the game neatly away. Harmon came to bat with no one on. He topped the ball, sending a slow roller to third baseman Brooks Robinson. Knowing he would have to leg it to beat out the hit, Killebrew strained himself to the limit. Just as he neared the first base bag he felt something give way in his right leg. He pitched forward, caught his toe on the bag and fell heavily, his short stocky body landing three or four yards beyond first base.

Fiery pain lanced up his right leg, and Harmon lay writhing on the ground. Trainer George Lentz, Elmer Valo and Lavagetto gathered quickly around him. After a long interval, Harmon was helped to his feet. He limped painfully into the dugout as excruciating darts of agony shot through his leg.

It was found that he had suffered a similar injury to the one he had endured in 1960. He had pulled a hamstring muscle in his right leg, and doctors estimated he would be out of action for three weeks.

The thought of three weeks of idleness appalled Harmon. He sat forlornly on the bench for a week, gently favoring his painful right leg when he moved. Every day Lentz examined the leg, and on each occasion Harmon told him it was feeling better. But Lentz was not encouraging about his return to the game.

Sitting on the bench drove Harmon almost to madness. He wanted badly to have a good year with the Twins—a better year than he had had in 1960—and an injury that kept him out of the lineup for any length of time was the last thing he could tolerate. Besides, it was agony watching his teammates struggle to win games while he was powerless to help them.

At the end of a week he went to Lavagetto. "The leg is feeling pretty good," he said optimistically. "I think I could at least pinch-hit today, if you want me to."

"We'll see," said Lavagetto cagily. He was determined not to let Killebrew play prematurely, for fear the injury would be aggravated and he would be lost for an even longer time.

"I'd like to be in the lineup when we open at home," Killebrew pressed.

"We'll see," was all Lavagetto would say.

On April 20 the Twins flew to Minneapolis for their home opener on the following day. That evening a huge "Meet the Twins" Banquet, arranged jointly by the Minneapolis and St. Paul Chambers of Commerce, was held at the Hotel Radisson in downtown Minneapolis. City officials and prominent citizens were present, and the entire team was honored as "the first major league ball team in the history of Twin Cities." It was a gay and flattering tribute that made all the members of the team feel that they were being accepted as a vital and important part of Twin Cities culture.

After the banquet, Joe Duffy, the Minnesota stadium manager, took Killebrew to Minneapolis station WTCN-TV and introduced him to Art Swift, the manager. Swift was full of ideas.

"Harmon," he said, "why don't you do a pregame show for us on TV? We could video-tape it on the ball field in advance of the game. You'll be the interviewer and you'll ask questions of other ballplayers—either on the Twins or on opposing teams. What do you say?"

Harmon looked doubtful. "Well, Mr. Swift, I've never done anything like that. I don't know how good I'd be at interviewing people."

"You'd be perfect. In fact, the program would be unique. Most of the time, a reporter interviews ballplayers. This program will feature a ballplayer interviewing other ballplayers. That's different. And it should go over, because you speak the players' language, you know the game. We're sure it will be a real good program."

"Well," said Harmon uncertainly, "I'd be willing to try it, I guess."

"Good," said Swift. "We'll work it out and I'll be in touch with you."

Swift had just left when a sportswriter came up and asked Killebrew whether he thought Ruth's record would be broken soon. It would have been understandable if Killebrew had blown his top over the persistent question, but to his credit he did not.

"It's possible that the record could be broken someday," he said. "With the hundred-and-sixty-two-game schedule, it gives modern batters a better crack at it."

"Who do you think might do it?" asked the writer.

It would have been a great story if Killebrew had named himself, but it was not in his nature to do so.

"Mantle, Colavito, Sievers or Lemon," said Harmon quietly.

The Twins' first sight of their brand new ball park was one that thrilled each of them. Metropolitan Stadium in Bloomington was spanking new and fresh-looking. It was a tidy little ball park with a seating capacity of only 40,000, but to a ball team loaded with power hitters it was a welcome sight.

"I think," said Harmon, "that you ought to be able to hit them out of here."

Most players agreed. The left and right field foul line measurements were 330 feet. Center field was 412. However, the distance from home plate to the wall along each foul line is not the true measure of a park's susceptibilty to the home run. It's the distance from home plate to left center and right center that counts, and this was in the area of 350 feet. Left center and right center are where most pull hitters, depending on whether they bat right-handed or left-handed, hit their longest drives. It is considered "home run alley" to the sluggers.

Metropolitan Stadium seemed ready-made for the long-ball hitter.

In batting practice before the home opener Killebrew attempted a few swings. But his leg felt stiff, and he could not get the power he needed into his swing. Finally he went back to the dugout, shaking his head.

"I guess I can't do it yet," he admitted.

"We'll wait a few days," said Lavagetto. "I'm as anxious to get you in there as you are, but we'll just have to sweat it out."

The opener itself proved more than enough to sweat out. Before a large crowd of new fans the Washington Senators, with a makeshift lineup of leftover players from the other teams in the league, beat the Twins 5–3.

The gloom was only momentary, however. By April 27 the Twins sported an 8–3 won-lost record and were only a few percentage points out of first place. Killebrew's leg was again feeling better, and he went to Lavagetto and told him he could play.

Lavagetto looked suspicious. "Let's wait," he said.

That day the Twins beat the Los Angeles Angels, 4–2, and took over first place with a 9–3 record. The Tigers were second with 8–2 and New York third with 7–4. The next day the Twins lost to the Angels, 6–5, in twelve innings and dropped to second place. The Detroit Tigers moved to the top, and the Yanks were third.

The following day Lavagetto finally relented. He put Killebrew back on first base, and Harmon got a single in four times up. But Los Angeles dumped Minnesota again, 4–1.

On April 30 the Twins took on the Chicago White Sox at Metropolitan Stadium. The game turned out to be a tense pitchers' battle between Bob Shaw of the White Sox and Jack Kralick of the Twins. At the end of the ninth inning the two teams were deadlocked, 2–2.

Killebrew was experiencing his best game since he returned to the lineup. He had collected two singles and a double in four times up and had raised his batting average over the .360 mark.

Neither team scored in the tenth inning, but in the eleventh the Sox rallied for three runs to give them a 5–2 lead. In the last of the eleventh Killebrew came to bat with no one on and made at least a token objection to the Chisox lead. He hit one of Shaw's low fast balls and golfed it into the left center field stands for his first home run of the 1961 season.

But the Twins went down to defeat, 5–3.

The following day Killebrew came up in the first inning with Allison on first as a result of a walk, and clouted a 370-footer into the left center field stands again. His second homer of the year paced the Twins to a 6–5 win.

On May 3 the Yankees came into Metropolitan Stadium. For Killebrew, it was one of those days when nothing seemed to go right. In the fourth inning, with Hector Lopez on first, Roger Maris hit a ground ball to Harmon at first base.

Killebrew scooped up the grounder, glanced at second and figured he had a chance to get Lopez going into second base. He heaved the ball and hit Lopez in the back with it. Both runners were safe.

In the seventh Killebrew booted a ground ball and set the stage for a four-run Yankee rally. When the frightful inning ended he went back to the dugout with his head hanging.

"My fault, Pete," he said to pitcher Pedro Ramos.

"Forget it," said Ramos. "How many games have you won for me with a home run, eh?"

In the last half of the seventh Killebrew partially atoned for his errors by hitting his third home run in three days into left field, but it was not enough to win. The Yanks romped away with a 7–3 victory.

In the dugout Killebrew was disturbed by the loss and the part he had played in it.

"My errors killed us," he said. "The trouble with the Yanks, you pay for your mistakes. They've got the guys who get on base and the wood to drive them in."

The next day the Yankees won again, 5–2, and then the Boston Red Sox came in. Reno Bertoia pulled up lame during batting practice, and Killebrew found himself back on third base for the opener with the Red Sox.

"Just a utility infielder," he said with a wry smile.

It turned out to be one of Killebrew's better games, and it won him a permanent place in the hearts of the new Twins fans. In the fourth inning he hit a bases-empty home run off Mike Fornieles—a 380-foot screamer over the right center screen. In the seventh he lashed a 410-foot drive over the center field fence with Len Green, who had singled, on ahead of him. They were his fourth and fifth of the season, and although they stirred up the fans considerably they were hollow achievements to Harmon. The Red Sox had managed to win in a slugfest, 11–9, and Harmon was again solemn in the clubhouse.

"So I hit a couple," he said. "But we lost—and they don't mean anything when you lose."

By this time Killebrew was engaged in his first television show. Before games he would interview players, and the discussion would be video-taped for use the next day. To his surprise, he found that he was good at interviewing. This was mainly due to the fact that he was talking baseball with baseball men, and both he and the person interviewed knew their subject. Mickey Mantle of the Yankees was one who was not surprised at Harmon's talent at interviewing.

"When Harmon talks to you about hitting, he makes

sense," Mantle said. "That's because he knows a little about hitting himself."

The interview worked both ways. Ballplayers were more content to be interviewed by one of their own than by a sports broadcaster. They talked the same language.

On the field, Killebrew remained at third base. On May 10 the Twins and Baltimore clashed in a contest that featured one dramatic big inning. The Twins, pulling out all the stops, scored nine runs in the second inning. Three home runs featured the uprising. Billy Gardner hit a homer with two on off starter Dick Hall. Zoilo Versalles clouted one with the bases empty off Hall. Killebrew smashed one 400 feet to the top row of seats in left field off reliefer Wes Stock with two on. The Twins won the game, 10–6.

This game tied the Twins with Baltimore for third place, just behind the Yankees in second and Detroit in first. So far the Twins were performing well for their new fans, and attendance at Metropolitan Stadium was highly satisfying.

Typical of the kind of ball the Twins were playing was a game with the Los Angeles Angels a few days later. This game rocked along for seven and a half innings, and at the end of that time the two teams were tied, 6–6. Ryne Duren was on the mound for the Angels, and Killebrew came up to face him in the eighth with no one on.

Duren, master of the blinding fast ball, decided to rely on his best pitch when facing the dangerous Killebrew. But his control was not too good. His first three pitches missed the plate and the count was three-and-oh.

Killebrew stepped out of the box and looked for the signal. It was the "take" sign. Harmon got back in the box and let a fast one cut the heart of the plate.

"Stee-rike!" cried the umpire, going up with his right hand in a dramatic gesture.

Killebrew got the "hit" sign on the next pitch. Duren tried

to curve him. As it broke, it looked to Killebrew to be one of those either-way pitches, so he swung and fouled it off. The count was now three-and-two.

Harmon decided that in this situation Duren would go to his favorite pitch, the overpowering fast ball. He did, and Killebrew was ready for it. He drove it high into the left field stands to give the Twins the go-ahead run. They went on to win the game, 13–6.

The next day Reno Bertoia, recovered from his pulled muscle, went back to third base, and Killebrew returned to first.

"It's nice to be able to play two positions," Killebrew grinned at his roommate, Allison. "That way there's always a place in the lineup for you."

"There'll be a place in the lineup as long as you keep hitting the way you are," said Allison.

Camilo Pascual pitched a four-hit masterpiece against the Chicago White Sox that day and shut them out, 5–0. Killebrew hit a triple to right center in the fifth and a double off the left field fence in the seventh. For the last fourteen games he had hit the ball at a blistering .404 pace, and he was leading all American League batters with a resounding .373.

And just to prove that he was no slouch in the field either, Killebrew made a scintillating play in the ninth inning to retire the Sox. Roy Sievers hit a ball with two out in the ninth to Bertoia at third. Reno's throw was low and in the dirt. Killebrew stretched for it, scooped it up, to end the game.

On May 18 the Twins and Kansas City Athletics engaged in a tight contest. In the first inning Versalles opened the game with a single off Ray Herbert. When Green grounded out, Versalles raced to second. Killebrew then punched a single into center to score Versalles. It was the twelfth straight game in which he had hit safely, and it was his twenty-second run driven in.

The game became a seesaw affair, and when the eighth inning opened the score was 4–3 in the Athletics' favor. There were two men on and one out when Killebrew came to bat with a chance to drive in the tying and lead runs.

Herbert studied Harmon carefully, then teased him with a tantalizing curve that broke outside. Killebrew started to swing, but checked it. Ball one.

The next pitch was a fast one and Harmon fouled it back against the screen, evening the count.

Herbert tried one inside and Killebrew let it go by for a ball. The next pitch was an either-way call, and the umpire decided it was a ball. There was a mild protest from Herbert, but the count stood at three-and-one.

Harmon took a second strike and, with a full count, Herbert went to the fast ball. It was a good pitch and Harmon swung. But he hit the ball on the ground and the Athletic infield turned it into a fast double play, leaving the runners stranded.

Lavagetto slapped a despondent Killebrew on the seat of his pants as he returned to the dugout.

"You can't do it every time," he said.

Despite this momentary failure, the fans were all for Killebrew. Once again the nickname "Killer"—which never did fit his mild personality—began to appear in the newspapers. There were chants from the stands when he came to bat, groans if he failed to deliver and great roars when he managed his specialty—a vaulting drive into the surrounding seats.

By now he was being deluged with requests to do commercials of all kinds. In time he made lucrative deals with a suit manufacturer, a breakfast cereal firm, a safety razor company and other businesses. As a result, his outside income mounted.

"You're going to need a business manager," said Allison.

"It's fantastic," said Killebrew, a little awed. "A kid from Payette!"

"You've come a long way, Harm," said Allison.

On May 20 Camilo Pascual pitched a five-hitter, winning 2–0. Killebrew accounted for both runs by hitting his ninth homer in the first inning, over the right field fence. In the clubhouse Pascual had a wide grin on his face.

"Harmon, he's my friend," he said. "He wins lots of games for me. Last year, so many I can't remember."

Killebrew just grinned sheepishly. "I don't hit many homers to right field. Maybe two or three last season."

He was now batting .363, best in the American League.

9

Manager Cookie Lavagetto was still not certain what position was best for Harmon Killebrew. He had done reasonably well at both first and third base, but his fielding still lacked the overall finesse demanded by major league baseball. What kept him in the game, of course, was his bat—for his hitting more than made up for any errors in the field.

"As long as he keeps swinging that big bat, he'll be somewhere in the lineup," Lavagetto said to a sportswriter. "But I would like to know just where he best fits into our infield."

While Lavagetto was mentally debating with himself about Killebrew, the Detroit Tigers came to town and whipped the Twins twice, 5–2 and 5–4. Although no one knew it at the time, it was the beginning of a disastrous skid that was soon to see the Twins in deep trouble. By May 30 the Twins had fallen to seventh place. But Killebrew was personally riding high. Between April 30 and the end of May he had hit twelve home runs in twenty-seven games and looked to be on his way to a fine slugging season.

On the first two days in June the Twins pulled two trades which they hoped would strengthen their club. On June 1 the Twins received second baseman Billy Martin from the Milwaukee Braves, giving the Braves infielder Billy Consolo and a bundle of money. The Twins also sent Paul Giel and Reno Bertoia to the Kansas City Athletics in exchange for out-fielder Bill Tuttle. It was an attempt by Minnesota to strengthen both their infield and their outfield, and with Bertoia gone it opened up third base for Killebrew.

"Looks like you're headed back to the hot corner, Harm," said Allison.

Harmon shrugged. Although he preferred first base, he was not one to make an issue of it.

"I'll play wherever Cookie wants me to," he said simply.

On June 2 another deal took place. This time the Twins optioned infielder Don Mincher to Buffalo in the Interna-tional League and received first baseman–outfielder Julio Becquer, who had been up once before, in exchange.

"We want to bolster our bench," was the way Lavagetto explained it. "Julio can play first base or the outfield. He'll be a handy man to have around."

The shuffling didn't exactly start a winning streak going. On June 4 the Tigers beat the Twins twice, saddling them with their fourteenth defeat in their last fifteen starts. Then the Yanks whipped them twice to make the record sixteen losses in seventeen games.

The Twins were now in eighth place.

Tension gripped the club. Rumors of more trades flew thick and fast. Top management wanted to post a good year in their first season in the Twin Cities, and the story that swept the club was that Cal Griffith wouldn't wait very long to make more moves.

He didn't. On June 6, at exactly 3:30 P.M., Lavagetto was replaced by Sam Mele, former American League outfielder and first baseman and more recently a coach for the Twins. But there was a strange element in this deal. Griffith made it plain that Lavagetto had not been fired. He had been sent on a week's "furlough." Mele was to run the club in his absence.

As a result of this unusual arrangement, a strange situation occurred that evening when the Yankees and Twins met at Metropolitan Stadium. At 8:30 P.M., in the third inning of the game, the Twins' Ron Henry was called out on strikes. Mele, in his capacity as interim manager, protested to umpire Bob Stewart with such vehemence that he was kicked out of the game. Ed Lopat, pitching coach, took over.

Thus in a period from 3:30 to 8:30 P.M., five hours, the Twins had three "managers"—Lavagetto, Mele and Lopat!

Not so strange was the fact that the Yankees beat the Twins again to make the Minnesota record a sorry seventeen losses in the last eighteen games. The next day the Yanks won again, and it was eighteen out of nineteen!

Killebrew, still bouncing between first and third, wasn't hurting particularly, even though the club was. His batting average had lost some of its loftiness, but he was still hitting .308 with twelve homers and was leading the Twins in batting.

Then, on June 8, the Twins broke their losing streak with a 3–1 victory over the Baltimore Orioles.

But the weird juggling of personnel on the club continued. On June 13 Lavagetto returned and took back the reins from Mele. That night Minnesota managed to scrape together an 8–6 win over the Kansas City A's for their returning manager.

It was a period of strangeness on the field too. The night after Lavagetto's return, Killebrew figured in a strange double play. It was the third inning and Camilo Pascual opened with a single. Billy Martin rapped a single to center, and Pascual stopped at second. The next Twin hitter was out, leaving runners on first and second, Killebrew up.

Harmon cut under a pitch and lifted a pop fly into short left center, and what happened after that was close to ridiculous. The A's shortstop, Dick Howser, raced into short center and signaled for the catch. But instead of catching it, he let the ball drop beside him.

Pascual and Martin held their bases, and they were sitting ducks when center fielder Gene Stephens raced in, picked up the ball, and threw it to Bertoia at third base to force Pascual. Bertoia then whipped the ball to second baseman Jerry Lumpe to get Martin. Killebrew wound up safe at first.

There was quite a rhubarb, with the Twins claiming that umpire Al Smith had invoked the infield fly rule, which would have automatically made Killebrew the only out, but Smith denied it and the play stood.

The Athletics won the game, 9–2—the start of another Minnesota losing streak.

Finally, on June 23, what seemed to be in the wind for so long actually happened. Cookie Lavagetto was fired. And this time Mele was officially named manager.

When Mele wrote out his first official lineup for a game with the Yanks on June 24, he put Killebrew on third base and the newly acquired Julio Becquer on first. A good crowd turned out at Metropolitan Stadium to see the Twins under their new pilot, and Mele pitched his ace starter, Pascual, in an attempt to assure a victory. The New Yorkers countered with Bob Turley.

The Yanks failed to score in the opening half of the first inning. In the Twins' half, Zoilo Versalles opened with a single off Bobby Richardson's glove back of second. Bill Tuttle was next up and Turley fed him a low one. Tuttle topped the pitch as Versalles streaked for second.

The ball dribbled down the first base line and Yankee catcher Elston Howard pounced on it like a cat. He fired the ball to first to get Tuttle, but Versalles rounded second and kept going. He was safe at third before the Yanks realized what had happened.

It was Killebrew's turn to bat. Turley pitched Harmon in

close and Killebrew fouled off the pitch. The next two balls were wide, but Turley came in with the fourth pitch. Killebrew swung and drove the ball between second and first for a single that scored Versalles with the first run of the game.

In the third inning Tuttle singled with one out to bring up Harmon again. The Killer looked at three wide ones as the count became three-and-oh. The next pitch was down the middle, but the take sign was on and Killebrew let it go by. With a three-and-one count, Turley threw a slider on the outside corner. Killebrew swung and the ball carried 380 feet over the left field screen, scoring two more runs and making the score 3–0.

In the seventh, Pascual, who was pitching one of his fine games, aided his own cause by smashing a double just inside the first base line. It looked as if he might be stranded on second, though, when both Versalles and Tuttle were easy outs. But up came Killebrew and drove a double off the left field screen to bring Pascual home with the fourth Minnesota run.

The game ended 4–0, with Pascual posting a six-hitter and Killebrew driving in all four runs.

The next day Mickey Mantle was talking to a Minneapolis sportswriter. "The way that Killebrew hits!" he said with enthusiasm. "For my money he's one of the best-looking hitters in baseball. What a beautiful swing he has!"

Apparently a lot of other American League players thought the same thing, for Killebrew by this time was getting a lot of player votes for the All-Star Game. On June 29, Killebrew's twenty-fifth birthday, Dick Cullum, sportswriter for the *Minneapolis Tribune,* hailed Killebrew as "one of the best young sluggers in the game." The remark was inspired by the fact that Harmon's latest home run streak had included ten in the last fifteen games.

By July 1, when the Twins met the Athletics at Kansas City, Mele had shifted Killebrew back to first base again.

"I'm trying to get my lineup set permanently," he told a writer. "And I've decided first base is Harmon's best position. Barring a lot of injuries or something, I think that's where he belongs."

The move satisfied Killebrew. "I'd rather play there," he said.

Minnesota had a fairly easy time of it against Kansas City. Going into the ninth, they were leading 5–2 with Jim Kaat pitching a good game. In the Twins' half of the ninth Kaat laced a double down the right field line. Then shortstop Dick Howser made consecutive errors on Versalles and Martin to load the bases. It brought up Killebrew, who promptly hit the first pitch over the left field wall for his twenty-third homer of the season and only the second grand slammer of his career.

Pressed for a statement in the clubhouse after the Twins had tucked away a 9–3 win, Killebrew was noncommittal as usual.

"Sure, it's a thrill. It's only the second time it ever happened to me."

Frank Lane, general manager of the Kansas City club, went away from the game shaking his head.

"That Killebrew," he said, "is worth four hundred thousand dollars right now on the open market. He's learned the strike zone. Man, how he's learned it!"

But despite all of Killebrew's heroics, the Twins failed to prosper. On July 4, the recognized halfway mark of the season, they were in eighth place with a 31–46 won-lost record, 18½ games behind the league-leading Tigers.

In the fourth of July doubleheader the Twins must have decided to do something about their sorry record. The Chicago White Sox had moved into Metropolitan Stadium, and despite the Twins' won-lost record, a good crowd showed up for the double bill.

The Twins won the first game, 6–4, on a ninth-inning bases-loaded homer by first baseman Julio Becquer. Dramatic as this come-from-behind victory was, it hardly measured up to the second game.

Jack Kralick, the Twins' left-handed dazzler, started against cagey Cal McLish of the White Sox. For seven innings the two hurlers had their rivals eating out of their hands, and nothing but a string of goose-eggs decorated the scoreboard.

Len Green was leadoff man for the Twins in the home half of the eighth. He measured one of McLish's slants for a single to open the inning. Bill Tuttle laid down a perfect sacrifice bunt to move Green to second. Kralick promptly connected for a single and drove in Green with the first run of the game.

But that wasn't all. Versalles, a fast man, laid down a bunt and beat it out for a single. That put men on first and second with one out.

Billy Martin rolled a slow one to Chicago shortstop Luis Aparicio. There was nowhere to go with the ball except to first base and Aparicio threw him out, Kralick going to third and Versalles to second. It brought up Killebrew.

Harmon had not been doing well over the past few days. He was oh-for-eleven when he faced McLish. McLish looked in for the sign, took his stretch, hesitated, then pitched. The ball was in tight. Ball one.

McLish threw again. Harmon swung and fouled it back against the screen. The next pitch was outside for a ball, and the following one caught the outside corner for a strike. Two-and-two.

McLish, working carefully, tried to curve Killebrew, but Harmon was expecting it. He swung and the ball shot like a dart into right center field.

It wasn't deep enough to go out of the park, and Killebrew legged it to first and made the turn to second. Chicago center fielder Jim Landis made a desperate effort to catch the ball and crashed into the fence. The ball ricocheted off the fence and rolled away.

Both runs had now scored and Killebrew, rounding second, headed for third. Landis, recovering, raced after the ball. Killebrew kept legging it and as he neared the third base bag he saw the coach waving him in. He turned third and raced for the plate.

Landis picked up the ball at this point and rifled it to the cutoff man, who whirled and fired it to the plate. But Killebrew slid in as the ball took a hop into the catcher's mitt.

It was his twenty-fifth home run of the season, and the first inside-the-park homer of his career!

Chicago scored two in the ninth, but the Twins won 4–2.

League competition took time out, then, so that the All-Star Game could be played at windswept Candlestick Park in San Francisco. Killebrew had been chosen on the team, but he was on the bench when the game got under way. As the National League All-Stars slowly built up their lead, pitchers like Warren Spahn, Bob Purkey and Mike McCormick held the American League batters to one hit in eight innings.

It was in the sixth that the one hit occurred. With no one on base, Killebrew was sent in as a pinch hitter. With one swish of the bat he drove a McCormick pitch into the stands for a home run. Killebrew then stayed in at third base for two innings, but he had no chances in the field. The game finally ended with the National League edging the American League, 5–4.

As the teams got back into action again in regular season play, Killebrew found himself hitting home runs at a rapid clip. By the end of July, when the second All-Star Game again interrupted regular league play, Killebrew was hitting a neat

.314, had 82 runs batted in and 32 homers. But the luckless Twins were mired in seventh place.

The second All-Star contest, played at Fenway Park in Boston, was called at the end of the ninth because of rain—a tie game, 1–1. Killebrew did not play in this game.

Through the months of August and September, Killebrew's home run production tapered off a little. He hit 14 more to end the season with 46, sufficient to win the home run title in most years. But this was the year that the M-Boys —Mickey Mantle and Roger Maris, of the Yankees—chose to make their assault on Babe Ruth's home run record. All of the screaming sports headlines went to them, and Killebrew, except in his home town of Minneapolis–St. Paul, went virtually unnoticed. Maris finally ended the season with 61 homers in the 162-game schedule as compared to Ruth's 60 in 154 games.

The Twins finished in seventh place, which didn't please the Minnesota brass at all. But they were highly pleased with Killebrew's 1961 record. In addition to the 46 home runs— which was the same number Orlando Cepeda of the San Francisco Giants hit to win the National League home run title— Killebrew batted .288 and drove in 122 runs. He finished eleventh in the American League's Most Valuable Player voting, the only member of the Twins to be named.

He went home to Payette, Idaho, that year knowing that he had a place on the team by virtue of his bat, but not at all sure what position he would play the following year.

10

During the winter months Harmon was visited in his Payette home by a writer for a national magazine. The writer was having a little difficulty getting answers to his questions, because Killebrew was so self-effacing and modest. Finally, almost in desperation, the writer asked him the obvious question: "What was your biggest thrill in baseball?"

Harmon grinned and walked out of the room, leaving the writer to study the Early American furniture in Killebrew's home. A moment later he came back with the baseball autographed by President Eisenhower.

"That was my biggest thrill," he said simply.

It was typical of Harmon to point to something outside his own achievements as his biggest thrill.

As in past years, Killebrew worked during the off-season at the Inter-Mountain Gas Company, mainly to keep himself occupied. Occasionally he found himself appearing at banquets and conventions, but he tried to hold such activities to a minimum since he enjoyed being with his wife and family and, by nature, was not cut out to do much talking—especially about himself.

In February, however, Harmon had something to talk about. Elaine presented him with his third child—this time a girl to join the two boys in the family. The couple named her Shawn, and her arrival immediately started talk about moving to a bigger house.

The next day after Killebrew became a happy father for the third time, he signed his contract with the Twins. It was reported at $34,000.

Almost immediately sportswriters began the questions.

"Maris hit sixty-one homers last year. Do you think you can better that this year?"

It was the kind of question Killebrew was inclined to evade.

"I don't know. It'd be pretty tough."

"What's your home run goal in 1962?"

"Well, I never really set a goal. I just try to have a good season."

"Any spring training aims?"

"Yes. I'm going to exercise and stretch my muscles," was his unexpected answer.

"Nothing else?"

"Oh, yes—one thing. I'm going to try to cut down on my strikeouts this year."

Harmon stayed home as long as possible before reporting to Orlando for the 1962 spring training season. He helped Elaine with the new baby, learning all over again the art of changing diapers and giving the infant her feedings, and when it came time to go, Elaine and her family stayed in Payette.

"We'll move in on you when you get to Minneapolis," she said.

When Killebrew reported at Tinker Field he was the highest paid player Cal Griffith had ever signed. Yet there was an ironic note to it all. Here he was the top-salaried man on the club, and he was a player *without a position!*

Griffith suggested on several occasions that Killebrew might be moved to the outfield, but Mele was thinking of him in terms of third base. Still, there was a red-hot second-year man named Rich Rollins battling for the third base job, and it was doubtful that Killebrew could beat him out for the position. In that case, Mele thought, first base was the answer.

It is always dangerous to move a slugger of Killebrew's proven ability from position to position for fear that the anxiety it engenders might affect his hitting. Mele wanted to get the problem settled as quickly as possible, and as a result Killebrew was looked at carefully in three positions—first base, third base and left field. As a glove man he proved to be adequate enough at all three positions, but outstanding at none.

The riddle of "what to do with Killebrew" persisted throughout spring training and was not definitely settled even as the team moved north. Killebrew, himself, wanted to play first base, but he was amenable to anything Mele wanted to try.

"I just hope it's settled by opening day," he said once. "I'd like to be able to play the season in one spot. Shuffling around during the season doesn't do you any good."

The question was virtually settled just before the season started when Griffith completed a trade with the Cleveland Indians. In a move to strengthen the infield, the Twins received first baseman Vic Power from the Indians in exchange for pitcher Pedro Ramos. In addition to Power, the Twins also obtained pitcher Dick Stigman.

This trade jelled the Twins' infield. Power, not only a good hitter but considered the best defensive first baseman in the league, was definitely assigned to the initial sack. Bernie Allen, a rookie, had been so impressive at second base he had taken that job away from veteran Billy Martin. Rich Rollins was assigned to third base and Versalles, much improved over the previous year, was placed at short. It seemed certain that this would be one of the better defensive infields in the league.

This infield alignment definitely settled the Killebrew problem. Harmon was installed permanently in left field. Bob Allison and Len Green completed the outfield.

Early in the 1962 season the famous "Killebrew split season" manifested itself again. In 1960 Harmon had gotten away to a slow start with only four home runs in the first half of the year, then had picked up speed in the second half. In 1961 he got off to a roaring start and tapered off in the last half. This time he got off to a slow start again.

Despite Harmon's slow beginning, however, the Twins did well in the early days of the 1962 season. Their tight infield, and a pitching staff that from the first showed great improvement, had them high in the first division. The four starters were Camilo Pascual, Jack Kralick, Jim Kaat and Dick Stigman, and the bullpen proved better than average with Frank Sullivan, Lee Stange and Ray Moore doing the fireman act. Baseball experts began to suspect that the Twins had the best pitching staff in the American League.

As far as the long ball was concerned, Killebrew had a frustrating first month. It was not until his thirtieth game that he finally managed to hit one out of the park. Then, in he next twenty-eight games he hit eleven.

Even so, as the season rolled into June, Killebrew was batting only .171. On June 7, in a game against the Kansas City Athletics, Mele benched him.

"You've gone oh-for-thirteen, Harm," he said. "A rest might do you some good."

Killebrew accepted the decision without question. He had been hitting poorly and the fans had been on him a little. To the Minnesota fans, Killebrew was the Killer when he was hitting home runs. When he wasn't, he was "Harmless Harm."

About this time Killebrew's frustration was deepened when Jim Lemon, who had been such a favorite adviser to Harmon, was sent to the Philadelphia Phillies. Harmon felt lost without the big lanky Lemon. Now he sat alone on the plane as the team flew from city to city, only occasionally joining his teammates in a songfest or talking with Bob Allison, with whom he still had a close association.

Killebrew sat out only four games during his benching and was back in left field on June 11 in a doubleheader against Chicago at Metropolitan Stadium. He was happy to be back in the game again, for he knew he needed as much experience in his new position as he could get. He was beginning to learn the intricacies of outfield play and was even beginning to enjoy roaming the spacious confines of left field.

Then, just as he was feeling secure in the outfield, first basemen Vic Power was injured in the first inning of a game with the Yankees—and suddenly Killebrew found himself at first base again!

The game turned out to be a seesaw affair. In the last half of the first inning, George Banks, who replaced Killebrew in left field, singled. Rollins then rapped a double to left field, sending Banks to third. Allison drilled a fast ground ball to Tom Tresh, the Yankee shortstop, and Tresh nailed Rollins going to third as Banks scored. Killebrew then slammed his eighteenth homer of the year off Whitey Ford to complete a three-run inning.

In the fourth and seventh innings Killebrew got singles, giving him three hits in three times up. Then came the dramatic ninth inning.

The Yanks were ahead, 9–6, and Whitey Ford was still working for the Bombers. Suddenly he tired, walking the first two Minnesota batters. A hurried call to the bullpen brought in relief specialist Luis Arroyo. Don Mincher greeted him with a long triple that scored two runs and made the score Yankees 9, Twins 8.

Things looked rather dim as the next two Minnesota hitters lifted easy pop flies, leaving Mincher still cooling his heels on third base. Then Arroyo got into grave trouble. He walked both Rollins and Allison, and suddenly the bases were loaded and Killebrew was striding to the plate.

An expectant roar went up from the crowd. Here was a situation ready-made for a Killebrew clout, and many of the fans were convinced that Harmon could pull the game out of the fire. Arroyo worked with extreme caution. A slider on the outside corner for a strike. A ball, wide. A fast ball that Killebrew fouled off. A second ball, in tight. Count two-and-two.

Arroyo curved the batter. It came in belt-high, breaking away. Killebrew brought the bat around. He hit nothing but air, going down on strikes and leaving the three anxious runners stranded!

On July 13 Killebrew reached a milestone in his hitting career. Minnesota was entertaining Washington at Minnesota. Pascual was pitching one of his fine games against the Senators, and when the Twins' half of the eighth rolled around the score was Minnesota 1, Washington 0.

Bill Tuttle opened the inning for the Twins with a rousing single to right field. Vic Power, now back at first base, laced one through the infield into center. Rich Rollins went down swinging to bring up Killebrew. Harmon delivered a home run that made the final score 4–0.

It was the one hundred fiftieth home run of his big league career.

A few days later another of those record-book games occurred. The Cleveland Indians were in Minnesota for a series, and the Twins' Dick Stigman was selected by Mele to make his first start. Barry Latman was on the mound for the Indians.

In the first inning the Twins loaded the bases against Latman with Bob Allison at bat. Allison unloaded them with a grand-slam homer.

Latman went out and Jim Perry came in. He promptly loaded the bases again to bring up Killebrew. Perry, thinking "this is where I came in," teased Harmon with a slider outside. Then he brushed the Killer back. Behind two-oh, Perry got one over the plate belt-high and Killebrew rode it into the left field stands.

It was the first time in major league history that two batters hit two grand slam homers in one inning.

Altogether, the Twins scored eleven runs in the first inning of that game on seven hits and four walks. Fourteen batters went to the plate.

Then, just for emphasis, Killebrew got another homer in the third with the bases empty. It was his seventh homer in seven games.

In the clubhouse afterward, Killebrew and Allison posed for pictures and endured the back-slapping congratulations of their teammates.

"How do you account for seven homers in seven games?" a reporter asked Killebrew.

Harmon shrugged. "I don't know. They just seem to be going out of the park. I'm not doing anything different. It's the same ball, the same bat and the same swing."

"Harmon knows the strike zone better this year than ever before," offered Sam Mele.

"But I swing the same," insisted Harmon.

"I've noticed you go in streaks, Harm," persisted the writer. "Anything to account for that?"

"Nothing I know of. It just happens, I guess."

The writer went away scratching his head. To a fellow reporter he said, "That Killebrew is a great guy. But he doesn't seem to want to talk much."

"He's just a nice modest kid," was the answer. "He tries hard all the time, and sometimes things begin to jell for him. He might go two weeks without another homer, then hit ten in a row. You never know."

11

The Twins were relentless in their pursuit of first place in 1962, and as August came around they were still riding high in the first division. There was even cautious talk of a pennant—this year, many thought, the Twins might outlast the Yanks.

On August 3 Killebrew kept the talk going when he made baseball history again. The Twins were in Detroit for an important series with the Tigers, who were also fighting for a berth in the first division.

In the fourth inning Killebrew came up to face Jim Bunning. Bunning fed him a fast ball on the inside edge of the plate, and Killebrew pulled it to left. The ball went up, up, up, as if it would never stop climbing. It landed high on top of the second-deck roof, 340 feet away, and bounced out of the park.

It was the first time any batter had ever cleared the second-deck roof.

Minnesota won the game, 7–4, and followed the next day with a 4–3 win in which Killebrew hit another homer of lesser dimensions.

By August 7, New York was in first place with 65 wins and 42 losses, and Minnesota was four games behind in second with 63–48. Killebrew had 29 home runs and was hitting .247.

But suddenly the Twins slumped. They slid into third place and by mid-August they were six and a half games behind the pace-setting Yanks. The Twins' fans were beginning to get impatient, and when Killebrew joined his teammates in the general slump the cries from the stands resumed.

"Harmless Harm! Harmless Harm!"

One day Sam Mele took Harmon aside. "You're in a slump, Harm, and I know why you're in a slump," he said.

Killebrew looked at the manager sharply. "I wish you'd tell me if I'm doing anything wrong out there."

"I've been talking to the umpires about you," Mele said. "You've been taking a lot of called strikes lately."

"I know I have," admitted Harmon.

"I think your trouble is that you're turning your head as the pitch comes in."

"My head?"

"Yes. You're not watching the ball as long as you should be. You turn your head as the pitch comes in—you pull it toward your left shoulder. Then your shoulder starts moving and you swing too fast. That's why you've been hitting a lot of balls on the end of your bat. And that's why you're taking called third strikes on the outside corner—because you're not getting as good a look at the ball as you would if you kept your head straight. What you're going to have to do is keep your head down, concentrate on the ball, and wait as long as possible before committing yourself with a swing at the ball. If you can work that out in a day or two, all right. Otherwise I'll have to bench you until you work it out in batting practice."

"I'll sure work on it," promised Killebrew, wondering if he was *really* jerking his head to one side as Mele said.

Killebrew worked at it, and on August 13 it seemed as if

he might have cured himself. The Yanks were again guests at Metropolitan Stadium.

In the first inning Len Green singled, went to second as Power grounded out, and waited there until Killebrew smashed a single to center to score him.

In the third the Twins loaded the bases to bring up Harmon, but this time the Killer fanned to end the inning.

In the fifth Green walked, Rollins singled him to third, and Killebrew drove a single to center to score Green. Allison then powered Rollins home with another single.

Despite all these heroics the Twins were still trailing 4–3 when the last of the eighth came around. But relief pitcher Bud Daley lost his control at this point and walked three batters—Green, Power and Rollins—in a row. That brought up Killebrew again with the bases jammed, the same situation in which he had fanned before.

Daley fed Killebrew a pitch in close. Ball one. Then he came in with a change-up and Killebrew swung too early. A fast ball was fouled against the screen and Daley's fourth pitch missed the outside corner. Two-and-two.

Daley started a curve at Killebrew and broke it over, but Harmon wasn't fooled. He sent a sinking liner into left field and Tony Kubek came racing in to get it. But the wicked drive caromed off his arm and rolled to the fence as three runs came in. The Twins beat the Yanks 6–4, with Killebrew getting four-for-five and driving in five of the six runs.

"I guess I stopped turning my head," he grinned after the game.

But the next day he was back in his slump again. The Twins managed to hang onto third place, but Killebrew went hitless in a doubleheader and did very little for the next week.

Suddenly the picture changed. The Twins emerged from their hitting slump, won a few games, and toward the end of

August found themselves only two games behind the league-leading Yankees. The fans and the Minneapolis–St. Paul papers began to speculate about a pennant.

On the last day of August the Twins were in Boston. Before the game Mele came up to Killebrew.

"Do you happen to know that you've hit a home run in every park except here in Boston this year?" he asked.

"No. I didn't know that."

"Well, you have. And it's kind of a shame, Harm, because this Fenway Park with its three-hundred-fifteen-foot left field foul line is made for right-handed hitters like you. How come you haven't got one here, anyway?"

It was a little bit of the needle and Harmon grinned.

"Maybe the pitching's been better here, Sam," he said softly.

"Why don't you try to complete the cycle today?" Mele suggested.

"I'll try my best," promised Killebrew.

Harmon made good on the promise. He hit his thirty-fifth homer of the season over the left field wall, although the Twins lost the game, 7–5.

The defeat was the beginning of disaster. The first part of September was a nightmare to the Twins. Killebrew suddenly stopped hitting again. The rest of the team began to sag with him, and on September 11 the Los Angeles Angels blanked the Twins, 9–0, to take over second place. The Angels were now four games behind the Yanks; the Twins were four and a half.

On September 12 Chicago whipped the Twins, 2–1, to put them five and a half games off the pace. With half a month of the season to go, it was a shattering blow to the Twins' title hopes.

The next day the Twins beat Chicago, 5–1, to move back into second place, but they were still five games behind the

Yankees. And because Killebrew was looking so bad at the plate, Mele benched him for two days.

"The rest will do you good," was his opinion. "It's been a long season."

Mele's remark about the rest doing Killebrew good proved to be the understatement of the year. When Harmon got back in the lineup on September 15 he embarked on one of the most amazing hitting streaks baseball has seen.

On that date the Twins met the Cleveland Indians. It was no contest, for the Twins rolled up twelve runs to Cleveland's two. But what sparked the game was Killebrew's hitting—he slammed two monstrous home runs, his thirty-eighth and thirty-ninth, to lead the Twins' attack.

"Looks like the rest did you some good," commented a sportswriter after the game.

"I really think it did," agreed Harmon. "I felt quicker and stronger up there. I got around on the ball better."

"Did you know that second homer you got wiped out a club record?" Mele asked him.

"No. What record was that?"

"The most homers ever hit by a Washington Senators' or Minnesota Twins' baseball team in one season was a hundred and sixty-seven. You tied that for this club with your first homer, and you beat it with the second."

But that was only the start of the fireworks. The next day Killebrew walloped his fortieth homer against the Indians to pace the Twins to a 4–3 victory.

There was no game scheduled on September 17, and on the next day Killebrew failed to hit. But on September 19 he went wild again. In a lopsided game with the Tigers, which the Twins won 12–5, Killebrew hit a home run in the fifth inning into the right field stands to break a 2–2 deadlock, then slammed another in the sixth over the left field screen. It was his third two-homer game of the season.

With Maris and Mantle having fallen off after their great splurge in 1961, Harmon began to see the chance of becoming the home run king of the American League—this time, all by himself. Norm Cash of the Detroit Tigers was his nearest competitor with thirty-nine homers, and Rocky Colavito of Cleveland trailed with thirty-seven.

On September 21, Killebrew added to his lead with a resounding 400-footer into the left field stands in the ninth inning of a game with the Baltimore Orioles—his forty-third of the year. On September 22 he hit still another, a three-run blast that accounted for all the runs the Twins scored in a 5–3 loss.

At this point in his incredible streak, Killebrew's last seven hits had all been home runs—two on September 15, one on the sixteenth, two on the nineteenth, one on the twenty-first and one on the twenty-second!

But it still wasn't over.

On September 23 Killebrew came to bat in a game against the Orioles with the score knotted at 2–2 in the eighth inning. There were two men on base at the time, and Chuck Estrada was on the mound for the Orioles. Killebrew lashed his first pitch over the left field screen—his forty-fifth round-tripper of the season.

No other man on the Twins' team had accounted for the big run so often, and during his unbelievable streak Killebrew was adding to his laurels. But in the same game in which he hit his forty-fifth homer, Killebrew also tied another less enviable major league record. He struck out for the one hundred forty-first time to tie the big league record set by Jake Wood, of the Detroit Tigers, in 1961.

On September 25 the Yankees officially clinched the American League pennant while Cleveland was thumping the Twins 5–1. But the one run scored by the Twins was Killebrew's forty-sixth homer of the year—this one off ex-Twin Pedro Ramos.

No games were scheduled on the next two days, and on September 28 the Twins whipped the Orioles, 11–5, to clinch at least a tie for second place. Killebrew hit only a single that day. But on the following afternoon, the last day of the season, he hammered out his forty-seventh and forty-eighth homers to lead the Twins to an 8–4 win over Baltimore that clinched second place alone.

Several records tumbled into Killebrew's lap as the 1962 season ended. The one he was least proud of was the strikeout record—in the last game of the season he whiffed for his hundred and forty-second time to set a new major league record for strikeouts. But when he hit his forty-eighth homer of the season—the last he got in 1962—it gave him several more enviable records. His forty-eighth circuit clout was his personal high and also a club high. Even more important, it gave him the home run title for 1962. It also represented his one hundred twenty-sixth run batted in, which was high for the league in that department.

But probably more remarkable than anything else was the fact that on September 15, when Killebrew returned to the lineup after his benching, he had had only thirty-seven homers to his credit. To capture the home run title, he had hit eleven home runs in the last eleven games!

Killebrew made his usual modest comment when sportswriters clustered around him to get his feelings about winning the home run and RBI titles.

"It's nice all right," he conceded. "But you'd better say that I won the triple crown—home runs, RBI's and strikeouts."

12

~~~~~~

The growing family of Harmon and Elaine Killebrew was by this time dictating a larger home, and between the end of the 1962 and beginning of the 1963 seasons the couple went house hunting. They found a pleasant home six miles away in Ontario, Oregon, on a two-acre plot of land, having decided definitely to live in the West and rent a flat in the Minneapolis area only during the baseball season.

Harmon kept himself occupied during the fall and winter months with a little pheasant and deer hunting and with his family interests. And, as always, he waited for that moment when he would again report to Orlando for spring training.

One day in early February Killebrew's phone rang, and it was Cal Griffith, calling from Orlando. In a brief conversation the general manager and Harmon reached an agreement on a 1963 contract calling for approximately $40,000. Winning the home run and RBI titles had paid off for Harmon in a better contract, but not all of it was based on the previous season's play. Griffith saw in Killebrew a potential even Harmon did not quite recognize—for Killebrew in 1962 was second only to Babe Ruth in home run frequency. Harmon had hit a home run every 13.1 times at bat. Ruth's record was 11.8.

Killebrew was always the last one to admit that he had a chance to crack Ruth's record or the new one set by Maris. In fact, he didn't even think in those terms. Over and over, to reporter after reporter, he would say, "I just try to hit the ball. I try to hit up the middle. I know I have the power to hit some of them out, but I never consciously try for a home run. They just come."

But the new contract reflected Cal Griffith's idea of the home run's importance in the scheme of things.

This time, when Killebrew reported to Tinker Field, he came with reasonable assurance that he would again be playing in left field. Although first base was still his favorite position, he had learned the intricacies of left field play, had become acquainted with the way the ball caromed off the walls of American League parks, and knew he could now do an adequate job there.

"You're not the fastest outfielder in the business, Harm," Mele said once, "but you get a good jump on the ball and you hang on to anything you reach."

"I'll play wherever you think it will do the club the most good," said Killebrew agreeably.

Spring training, 1963, turned out to be a near-disaster for the Twins. They lost game after game in the exhibition schedule, and the club's weak hitting had Mele concerned. No one seemed to be getting hits, especially when they counted, and Killebrew was one whose bat had lost its charm.

Then, one day, Killebrew slipped on a soft spot in the infield as he ran out a grounder and felt a sharp pain tear through his right knee. It was so severe that he almost collapsed, and Mele and the trainers ran onto the field to help him back to the dugout. Dr. Bill Proffitt, the team physician, diagnosed the injury as a bad sprain, and from then on, during each day of the spring training season, Killebrew taped the knee tightly before venturing onto the field.

All through the exhibition schedule the twisted knee not only slowed Harmon down but also affected his swing at bat. He took extra batting practice, despite the fact that the knee bothered him constantly, in an effort to improve his hitting.

But the new season seemed jinxed for him. A few days later he slipped again and sprained an ankle. Still he insisted on taking extra batting practice, gritting his teeth against the pain.

"I think I'd better rest you a few days," said Mele, but Killebrew persuaded the manager to let him play.

"I've got to work the soreness out," he said. "If I stop I'm afraid it will tighten up."

Mele went away shaking his head. "The kid's got a lot of guts," he said to himself.

So Harmon, by his own insistence, stayed in the lineup during almost the entire spring baseball schedule, even though he failed to help the stumbling Twins. When the Grapefruit League season ended, the team that had finished in second place in the American League the year before had won only seven games and lost twenty. As an indication of how helpless they were at the plate, there was one stretch of thirty-six innings during which they scored only four runs.

It was a sorry record, and it persuaded the experts to shy away from predicting a pennant for the Twins. Minnesota was picked to finish anywhere from second to fourth.

As the team moved north for its opener, concern for Harmon's twisted knee grew. There was now fluid forming on the knee, and Killebrew lived in constant pain. Dr. Proffitt expressed the view that Harmon probably would not be able to play in the American League opener. But just before the opening contest, fluid was drained from his knee, and by morning of the getaway game he was feeling much better.

The Twins took on the Cleveland Indians at Bloomington in their opener, presenting substantially the same lineup that had won them second place the year before. The batting order was Len Green in center, Vic Power at first, Killebrew in left, Bob Allison in right, Bernie Allen at second, Earl Battey catching, George Banks substituting for an injured Rich Rollins at third, and Zoilo Versalles at short. Their best pitchers were Camilo Pascual, Jim Kaat, Dick Stigman and Ray Moore, with Pascual scheduled to work the opener.

Cleveland won the opener, 5–4, and Killebrew, who went hitless, limped through the game on his gimpy knee. Because he favored the painful knee, Killebrew found his swing at bat was still restricted. What speed he had in the outfield was sharply curtailed. He wanted badly to remain in the lineup, but not to the extent of hurting the team's chances, so he made no reference to the pain he felt. But it was obvious as far up as the last row in the stands that he was not playing at 100 per cent of his capacity.

Killebrew remained in the lineup for the second game with Cleveland the following day. This time he did better. The Twins were leading, 4–3, in the eighth inning when Killebrew stepped to the plate to swing against Barry Latman. He swung hard against a Latman curve and the injured knee twanged with pain—but the ball soared into the left field stands for Killebrew's first home run of the new season. It gave the Twins an insurance run and they won the game, 5–3.

In the clubhouse the usual number of reporters gathered around Killebrew.

"For a guy with a bad knee, you clobbered that one pretty well," he commented.

"Well, I guess I just happened to get hold of it," said Harmon.

"You know, Harm," the writer went on, "this year you hit your first homer on April tenth. Last year you didn't get it until April twentieth. Does that indicate anything to you?"

Killebrew just smiled. He knew the writer was fishing for a statement about how a good start might help him to break the records of Ruth and Maris.

"I don't think it means a thing," he said honestly. "I'm a streaky hitter. I might start early this year and then fall flat. You just never know."

The Twins lost a couple after that game and then went to Kansas City to meet the Athletics. Here the entire Twins team put on a sad exhibition, and Killebrew was among the saddest of all. As the A's defeated the Twins, 5–4, pitchers Diego Segui and Orlando Pena posted thirteen strikeouts against Minnesota. Killebrew accounted for almost a third of that total by fanning four straight times.

And each time his knee hurt!

That was enough to convince Mele that Killebrew, for all his grit in trying to play, was not right. He benched him the next day to rest the knee, installing in his place rookie Jim Hall.

Harmon's sore knee was again puffed with fluid. It pained him during the day, and it kept him awake at night. He had to be careful with every step he took, for fear he would twist it more.

Dr. Proffitt worked diligently to get Killebrew back in action. The fluid was drained again, cortisone injections were made, the whirlpool treatment prescribed. Gradually the soreness left, and by May 11 Harmon thought he could play again.

"I'd like to try it again," he told Mele.

"Okay, you're in. But be careful."

Mele put Harmon back in the lineup in left field. But he played only five innings and retired in favor of Hall. The next day he sat on the bench again because an all-night rain had made the outfield slippery, and Mele was taking no chances of reinjuring Harmon's tender knee.

Killebrew returned to the lineup on May 14 and played the entire game. New York beat the Twins that day, 2–1, and Killebrew went hitless. Harmon sat in front of his locker shaking his head after the game.

"Did the knee bother you much?" asked a sportswriter.

"No. Not much. It's just that my rhythm is all off. It's just gone, that's all. It looks like I'll have to start all over again."

"Don't worry," said Mele. "It won't take you long to get your timing back as soon as you can stay in the lineup every day. Not as long as it does in the spring when you've been away for four or five months."

"I hope I get it back soon," said Killebrew disconsolately. "I'd like to be able to help this club."

The Twins needed all the help they could get. They were now in the American League cellar with a record of eleven wins and twenty losses, an embarrassing position for a team that had aspired to the pennant the year before.

Slowly Harmon regained his batting form, and when he did it sparked the rest of the team. In a four-game series with Cleveland, for example, the Twins hammered out twelve home runs. Mele had a cluster of reporters around him when the series ended.

"Give a lot of the credit to Harm," he said. "He fires up the team when he's in there. The boys feel they can do it with Killebrew in the lineup. Their whole attitude becomes more aggressive. They figure all the pressure is on the pitcher, and they really go after him."

This was a high tribute to Killebrew, because it made plain that Harmon's contribution to the Twins was not exclusively his ability to hit the ball out of the park. He was also an inspiration to the rest of the team, a spark plug that put more spirit in the play of other players by the very fact that he was one of them.

Spurred by Harmon's leadership, the Twins started to

climb in the standings, and on May 24 they clashed with the Chicago White Sox in an important home game. It turned out to be a tense cliff-hanger all the way.

Chicago grabbed a 2–0 lead in the second inning. In the last of the fourth Vic Power slashed a double down the third base line for the first hit off Ray Herbert. Herbert bore down on Killebrew. He got a fast strike across, then befuddled the Killer with a change-up for strike two. But Killebrew hit the third pitch into left field for a single that brought Power home with the Twins' first score.

In the last of the fifth, trailing 2–1, the Twins really went to town. Rich Rollins singled to right. Versalles followed with another single. Bernie Allen dropped a Texas leaguer into left and the bases were loaded.

Shaken by the sudden attack, Herbert walked Len Green to force in the tying run. Power flied to short right and the base runners could not move.

Killebrew stepped into the batter's box with all the bases occupied by eager Twin runners. Herbert stooped, got some resin on his fingers, and peered in for the sign. Then he delivered a curve, inside and tight. Ball one.

Harmon stepped out, got dirt on his hands, wiped his hands on his trousers, and took his place in the batter's box again. Herbert came in with a slider that caught the corner. One-and-one. The third pitch brushed the Killer back, but the fourth was a soft curve that hung.

Killebrew drove it into the right center field bullpen for his fifth homer and first grand-slammer of the season.

With a 6–2 lead it looked as if the Twins would coast home. But Chicago would not play dead. They scored one in the seventh to make it 6–3, and this score held through the eighth. When the White Sox came to bat in the ninth, Mele took Killebrew out of the ball game and put Jim Hall in left field as a defensive measure.

"You've given us the ball game with your bat," he said to Harmon. "We'll let Hall defend it."

But Chicago went on a rampage in the top of the ninth, scoring three runs and tying the game, 6–6!

In the last of the ninth the Twins managed to get a man on base with two out, but it didn't look promising. Hall, substituting for Killebrew, was at bat—and Mele couldn't help but wish he had Harmon in there instead.

But Hall proved equal to the challenge. He walloped a game-winning homer into the left field stands. Final score: Minnesota 8, Chicago 6.

In the clubhouse Mele was shaking his head with wonderment.

"A crazy game," he said. "I take our biggest offensive threat out of the lineup and put Hall in for defense. Then Hall's the guy who hits a homer to win the game for us."

"Better watch out, Harm," kidded Allison. "Hall might take your job away."

"Anything's possible," said Harmon—and meant it.

13

By early June the Twins had regained some of the respect of the rest of the league by climbing to fifth place. Most of their success was due to their hitting, particularly the long ball. Homers were producing 45 per cent of the Twins' runs. By June 12 Minnesota found itself in fourth place, only two and a half games out of first. Chicago was leading the league, New York was second and Baltimore third.

About this time the Twins arrived in the clubhouse one day to see a gymnastic bar set up in the dressing room. The players gathered around it, curious, and were discussing the possible uses of the bar when manager Mele strode up.

"That's for exercising," he said bluntly. "Anybody wants to use it is welcome, but we put it up for Killebrew. He wanted it."

Bob Allison walked over to Killebrew's locker. He had a puzzled expression on his face.

"What's the idea of the bar, Harm?"

"I asked Mele if I could have one," Harmon said. Then he looked a little sheepish and added, "I want to build up my strength."

Allison's jaw dropped. *"You* want to build up your strength?" he exclaimed. "You're out of your mind, Harm. You're already the strongest man in baseball!"

"Well, I don't know about that. Anyway, you can't have too much strength in this game."

Killebrew reached into his locker and withdrew a book which he handed to Allison.

"I've become interested in isometrics lately," he said. "I've been doing a lot of reading on the subject."

Allison looked at the book, wonderment still on his face. It was *Functional Isometric Contraction,* by United States weight-lifting coach Bob Hoffman.

"Holy smokes!" said Allison. "What *is* this stuff?"

"Well, it's a theory for building your strength," said Harmon. "It advocates a method of static strength development."

"And with this you're gonna get stronger than you are?" asked Allison, still amazed.

"I hope so," said Killebrew simply.

Killebrew worked religiously on the bar whenever the Twins were at home, chinning himself and doing other exercises designed to strengthen arm, neck and shoulder muscles. Rich Rollins also became greatly interested in the theory of isometrics, and the other players took turns on the bar, more out of curiosity than any great dedication.

It seemed, on June 18, that Killebrew's work on the bar was paying off. In a game against Chicago at Metropolitan Stadium, he helped defeat the White Sox, 5–3, by blasting a home run that went 432 feet and landed in the thirty-ninth row of the bleachers in left field. Newspapers promptly tabbed it as the "Granddaddy of them all." While this may have been stretching the truth to some extent, the homer was in any event one of Killebrew's most prodigious.

A week later Harmon hit another off Jim Bunning of Detroit that went almost as far. It gave the Twins a 1–0 win over the Tigers.

"Maybe there's something to this isometric stuff," conceded Allison.

During the last week in June the Twins won seven straight, but the problem they faced was the fact that the other three teams in contention for the pennant were also winning. By June 28 the Twins were still three games out of first and resting in fourth place. New York now had the lead, Chicago was second and Boston third.

Then, just when the team seemed headed for better things, disappointment struck. In the second game of a July 4 doubleheader with the Tigers—which the Twins lost, 5–3 and 3–1—Killebrew put on a burst of speed trying to outrun a double-play ball and pulled the hamstring muscle in his left leg again. The injury crippled him in both legs, for his right knee, while improved, still bothered him.

In the clubhouse a glum Killebrew watched as trainer George (Doc) Lentz examined the new injury.

"These hamstring muscles take a long time healing," he said. "I'd say he'll be out for a while."

"How long?" asked Mele.

"Hard to say," said Lentz. "Indefinitely is a good word."

"It's not too painful," said Killebrew hopefully. "I'd hate to miss any games."

"We'll take no chances," was Mele's comment.

Wally Post went in for Killebrew the next day. It was another doubleheader, and in the ninth inning of the first game Mele said, "You think you can pinch bat, Harm?"

"I think so. The leg feels pretty good."

"Okay. Go on in."

Killebrew struck out, but he was encouraged by the fact that the leg pained very little and asked Mele if he could play in the second game.

"If you think you can do it, Harm," said the manager, "I'll put you in."

Mele left Killebrew in the second game for six innings, during which time he struck out three times.

"Maybe I *am* favoring the leg," Harmon admitted afterward. "And I guess it's doing something to my swing."

On July 9 the All-Star Game interrupted regular league play. The National Leaguers won, 5–3, in a game played at Cleveland's Municipal Stadium. Killebrew saw limited action, batting only once and going hitless, but when the regular season resumed he was back in the Minnesota lineup again.

July 19 was a red-letter day in Harmon's career. In a thirteen-inning game that Minnesota lost, 6–5, Killebrew hit his twenty-second homer of the year. But there was something special about this one—it was the two hundredth of his major league career.

When a reporter asked him how he felt about this milestone in his hitting career, Harmon said, "It's a thrill, all right, every time you hit a homer—and hitting number two hundred is something extra. But homers aren't the main thing in this game. Winning is the main thing, and when you don't win the homers lose a lot of luster."

Two days later Killebrew hit his twenty-third homer, and when the end of the month came he still had his twenty-third. Bob Allison now led him, having poled twenty-five.

As the days passed, a lot of good-natured rivalry sprung up as the "home run twins" battled for the league lead. Sports writers insisted on asking Killebrew the obvious question.

"Do you think Allison will take the home run championship away from you this year, Harmon?"

Killebrew thought it was a foolish question, because he had long ago schooled himself not to think of home runs as a particular objective—and he had virtually worn himself out trying to tell people this.

"Whether you're competing with a player from a rival club or your own," he explained patiently, "you just go out and do the best you can. Personally, I hope Bob hits a hundred. The chances are we'll win ball games that way. That's the only important thing."

Allison agreed with Killebrew. In their room one night on the road, Allison said, "Why does everyone think that a home run is the biggest thing in baseball? They can't seem to understand that winning the game is the real objective, whether you do it with a single or a homer."

Harmon shrugged. "I've been trying to say that for years," he replied.

In early August Killebrew's home run production picked up and he promptly tied Allison at twenty-five. But his home run pace was slower than 1961 when he hit forty-two and 1962 when he hit his league-leading forty-eight.

On August 7, with Minnesota trailing the Los Angeles Angels, 4–2, in the eighth inning at Bloomington, the Twins started a rally. Rollins and Power hit consecutive singles with one out to bring up Killebrew. Those two hits and the threat of Harmon at the plate brought the Angels' manager, Bill Rigney, to the mound for a conference with his pitcher, Ken McBride. After a short discussion on how to pitch to Killebrew, Rigney left McBride in.

The strategy, of course, was to force Killebrew to hit one on the ground for a double play. The Angels figured that anything hit at normal speed to the infield could be converted into a twin killing because of Killebrew's slowness in getting down to first.

McBride tried to keep the ball low, hoping Killebrew would top it with his swing. The first two pitches were too low, for balls. McBride aimed the next one at the inside corner and nipped it for a strike. Then he got another one too low for a three-and-one count.

McBride reared back and threw a fast one down the middle and Killebrew took it for strike two. Killebrew stepped out of the box and studied McBride for a moment. He reasoned that the pitcher wouldn't dare feed him another fast ball with the count full—it was almost sure to be a breaking pitch.

Harmon stepped back in, crouched slightly over the plate. When the pitch came in, Killebrew saw he was right. The ball began to break and Harmon measured it carefully with his swing. He powered it high into the left field stands to put the Twins ahead, 5–4. It was his twenty-sixth homer of the year and broke the tie that existed with Allison. The Twins went on to win the game, 9–4.

On August 10 Killebrew had twenty-six home runs with forty-eight games to play. It was questionable now whether he could reach his 1962 total or whether he would be able to retain his home run title. And the questions came again.

"Do you think you'll get forty-eight again this year?"

"Do you think you'll get the home run title again?"

Killebrew patiently explained it. "What helped last year is that I hit eleven home runs in the last eleven games. But you can't figure on doing that sort of thing often. I haven't had a hot streak like that all this year. I don't remember hitting more than one home run in a game this year. So I'm not making any predictions."

The next day the team played Boston, and Killebrew went hitless. After the crowd had left the stands, Killebrew went out and took twenty minutes of extra batting practice. Mele, talking to a sportswriter, said, "I wish I knew what was wrong with Harm. He's getting some homers, sure, but he hasn't been getting a good piece of the ball all year—not like he was last year, anyway."

"He doesn't have to get a good piece of it," said the writer. "With his strength he can power the ball out of here on a half-swing."

"I know. And you're right. But he's still not swinging the way he used to swing."

"Is it that head business?" asked the reporter. "Is he turning his head too quick, not following the pitch?"

"I've been watching him," said Mele. "No, I don't think that's his trouble. The one thing it might be—and I hate to think of it—is his knee."

"It's still bothering him?"

"Yes. Not enough to keep him out of the lineup, but he may be favoring it a little and it's thrown off his swing. The knee has never been quite right since he twisted it down in Orlando."

Killebrew knew this to be true. He was taping the knee heavily before games, and there had been some pain evident all season long. But he was not one to languish on the bench if he could so much as walk up to the plate, and he wanted to stay in the lineup as much as possible.

August was not a highly productive month for Killebrew and by the twenty-eighth of the month he had only twenty-nine home runs. And, as if it had been psychologically timed, it was right during this difficult dry spell that Commissioner Ford Frick asked Killebrew what he thought of major league baseball!

The question about baseball was put in the form of a survey which the Commissioner's Office made of ballplayers in the major leagues. Each player was asked for a statement on what the game of baseball had done for him.

Killebrew wrote: "Signing a big league contract was one of the big thrills of my life and one of the smartest things I ever did. It meant heartache, frustration, disappointment, hard work and oftentimes painful injury. But all of these things have made playing in the big leagues twice as sweet. By my connection with the game I have met some of the most important people of our time—a President, Vice President and many cabinet officers. My earnings have enabled me to provide a better home for my family sooner than I would have been able otherwise. During the season I've been able to live and travel first class, and through baseball I was able to get a job as a radio and TV broadcaster."

Killebrew's reply to Frick's question was so honest and forthright that it was selected for publication by the *Minneapolis Tribune.*

On August 29, one of the most memorable days in the history of the Twins occurred. The team was in Washington to play the Senators in a doubleheader, and what happened was an awesome slaughter that had the capital city talking for days.

The Twins beat Washington twice, 14–2 and 10–1, but that alone was not the important thing. It was the way they did it that upset the record book. The Twins hit twelve home runs that day in the biggest display of power they had ever put on. And Killebrew contributed a substantial share to the carnage.

In the first game, Killebrew faced Pete Burnside in the fifth inning and lined a 450-foot home run into the 50-foot-high center field seats. Then, in the sixth, he hit another off Ron Moeller to climax a big six-run inning. He also had a single in the game.

In the second contest, Killebrew hit another off Burnside, who was in as a relief pitcher.

In the process of completing their slaughter of the hapless Senators, the Twins set three records and tied one. The doubleheader, coupled with previous games, put the following records into baseball's record book.

The Twins broke the major league record for most home runs in three consecutive games with fifteen.

They broke the major league record for most homers in four games with seventeen.

They broke the American League record for most home runs in five consecutive games with eighteen.

They tied the major league record for one game with eight homers in the opener, held by the Yanks in the American League and Milwaukee, Cincinnati and San Francisco in the National League. The eight home runs included Killebrew and Power with two each, and Allison, Hall, Allen and Rollins with one apiece.

But not all the news was good. While in Washington, Killebrew consulted Dr. George Resta, the Senators' team doctor and a good friend. The doctor X-rayed Killebrew's bothersome knee and was appalled at its condition.

"I don't know how you've been able to play on it," he said frankly. "It must have taken a lot of courage. There are a great many loose fragments in the knee area. You'll never have relief until you have it operated on and the fragments removed. That's what I advise."

Killebrew nodded gloomily. "It's been bothering me right along," he admitted. "I guess I'll have to have it done. After the season, though."

As the final month of September opened, the American League awakened to the fact that there was a red hot race going on for the home run championship. Killebrew, who slammed his thirty-fourth on September 2 against Chicago to help beat them, 6–2, found that Dick Stuart, of the Boston Red Sox, had passed him with thirty-five. The sportswriters, ever alert to drama, played up the big race in black sports headlines. Killebrew, the title holder of the previous season, was in danger of being dethroned by a young man in Boston whose bat had suddenly become alive! It wasn't Mantle or Maris or Colavito who was threatening, but a player who up to this year had not been considered a particular threat to the long-ball hitters of the league.

Killebrew and Stuart remained neck-and-neck throughout

the first week and a half of September. On September 11 Harmon was one home run behind Stuart, but in a game with the Indians on that date he hit his second grand slam of the year to pace the Twins to a 9–3 win. The round-tripper tied Dick Stuart at thirty-eight.

In the next few days Stuart collected a couple of homers while Killebrew failed to get the ball out of the park, and Harmon found himself two behind again. One day Harmon and Cal Griffith met on the field.

"Knee still bothering you?" Griffith asked.

"Yes. It's rough at times."

"I think you'd better take the doctor's advice and have it operated on this fall," Griffith said.

"I think I will," replied Killebrew. "I don't want to go through another season like this one."

The painful knee handicapped Killebrew in his home run race with Stuart. Each time he swung at the ball it pained him, and the very fact that he knew it would hurt with each swing made him cautious and changed his rhythm. Still, by sheer grit, he stayed close behind the pace set by Stuart.

On September 17 Killebrew was still two behind Stuart. The Detroit Tigers came into Minnesota for a series, and the Twins' Dwight Siebler hooked up in a pitching duel with the Tigers' Hank Aguirre. For five innings the teams rocked along in a scoreless tie. Then, in the sixth, Killebrew caught one of Aguirre's slants and drove it into the left field seats for his thirty-ninth of the year. The blow not only started the Twins on a 3–1 conquest of the Tigers, but put him only one homer behind Stuart's forty.

The next day the Twins met Detroit again. Killebrew was hitless the first time up. Before he came to bat again the scoreboard flashed the news that Stuart had hit his forty-first home run!

Killebrew went to bat and flied to center, but later in the

game he blasted a long drive off Willie Smith for his fortieth homer of the year.

Killebrew was again one behind!

In the clubhouse after the game, Killebrew attempted to answer the eager questions of the sportswriters.

"You think you'll catch Stuart?"

"I don't know. How can you say?"

"Do you think there's a chance Stuart will taper off?"

Killebrew shrugged. "I have no control over what Stuart does," he said logically. "All I can do is keep swinging."

"You have one more game with the Tigers, then you go to Boston," said a writer. "It looks like a face-to-face showdown between you and Stuart."

Killebrew grinned. "Showdowns don't always come off the way you think. Probably neither of us will hit a thing."

It was a typical Killebrew comment.

Detroit defeated the Twins, 8–6, in thirteen innings the next day, and Killebrew failed to get his tying home run. Stuart didn't hit one either, so as the Twins moved into Boston to meet the Red Sox the home run score was still Stuart forty-one, Killebrew forty.

The newspapers buzzed with speculation as the two teams prepared to meet each other on September 20. It was so close to the end of the season that a good day for either player might decide the home run title right then. Boston fans were poised to see the showdown.

Then, as if to prolong the suspense, it rained on September 20 and the game was postponed. That set up a big Saturday doubleheader for the following day and the fans came out in thousands to see the two top sluggers of the American League in a long day of showdown baseball.

As Killebrew dressed in front of his locker before the game, Howard Fox, the Twins' road secretary, came up.

"How do you feel, Harm?" he asked.

"Fine."

"The knee okay?"

"Just fair."

"I had a dream last night," said Fox, grinning. "I hope it comes true."

"What was it?" asked Killebrew.

"I dreamed you hit six home runs," said Fox.

Killebrew laughed. "There isn't much chance *that'll* come true."

The Boston Red Sox, doing everything possible to keep Killebrew's bat silent, threw their ace pitcher, Bill Monbouquette, into the first game.

Killebrew came to bat in the first inning with the bases empty. Monbouquette, ever aware of the fine target the left field wall makes for right-handed hitters at Fenway Park, tried to keep the ball outside. If he could keep Killebrew from pulling the ball, he could probably keep him from hitting it out of the park.

His first pitch was too far outside for a ball. The next nipped the corner for a strike. On the third pitch he threw a change-up, and Killebrew swung too early. One ball, two strikes.

Harmon twisted his right foot into the dirt and waved his bat at the pitcher. After the change-up, Killebrew decided, there would be the fast ball—and there was. Killebrew drove it over the inviting left field wall for a homer.

The home run race between Killebrew and Stuart was now tied at forty-one each!

A thunderous roar greeted him as he rounded the bases and shook hands with almost everyone in the dugout. Although the crowd was rooting for Stuart, they recognized the fact that Killebrew's achievement promised a long afternoon of excitement. There were still seventeen innings of baseball remaining, and with the homer count tied, anything could happen.

By the time the fifth inning came around the Twins had grabbed a 7–2 lead. Monbouquette had left the game, and Pete Smith was now pitching for Boston. Smith was determined not to become a Killebrew victim, as Monbouquette had been, and laid off the fast balls. He curved Harmon inside, and he curved him outside—and then he curved him over the heart of the plate, and Killebrew blasted it into the stands for his forty-second home run!

An ominous roar came from the stands this time, for now Harmon was ahead of Stuart by one!

The partisan fans began to chant as Stuart came up to face the Twins' Lee Stange in the sixth. The stands rocked with, "We want a homer! We want a homer!"

Stange worked on Stuart carefully—a little too carefully, because he got behind in the count. With the count three-and-one, Stange tried to slip a fast one by. Stuart rapped it into the seats and the home run race was tied up again at forty-two!

In the press box one reporter grinned at another. "We were hoping for a showdown, and it looks like we really have one," he said.

"Don't start writing your story yet," said the other. "Anything can happen."

By the eighth inning the Twins had built a lopsided lead. Arnold Early was on the mound when Killebrew batted for the last time. Early tried everything in his bag of tricks, but Killebrew hit one out of the park anyway—his third home run of the game!

The home run score was now Killebrew forty-three, Stuart forty-two.

In the clubhouse between games the Twins players hardly took notice of the fact that they had won the first game, 13–4. All they could talk about was Harmon's three four-basers that had given him the lead in the home run race.

"You've got him on the run, Harm!" said Allison.

"Don't be too sure," said Killebrew. "Stuart's only one behind and he can even that up next game. One big swing will do it."

The second game, as far as the score was concerned, was an opposite of the first. This time Boston got away to a flying start, and the Twins' bats were curiously silent. Lanky Gene Conley was on the mound for Boston, and he was throwing an assortment of stuff that baffled the Twins' batters.

Stuart, however, was having his own personal troubles with a succession of Minnesota pitchers, and it looked as if the day would end mildly after the bombardment in the first game. But in the sixth inning Killebrew drove his fourth homer of the day into the stands with the bases empty to make the homer score Killebrew forty-four, Stuart forty-two!

The Twins lost the second contest, 11–2, but the defeat didn't dampen their spirits any. Killebrew was the big hero of the day. Teammates and sportswriters crowded around him, asking questions and offering congratulations—for his performance had virtually clinched the home run title.

"I wish," said Allison wistfully, "that I had a sore knee like Harm does."

"Everybody should have a sore knee like Killebrew!" Mele crowed happily.

"Did you ever hit four homers in one day before?" a sportswriter asked.

"No," said Harmon. "This was my best power day ever. I've never hit four home runs in one day before in the majors, minors, high school or sandlot."

Killebrew posed for pictures as photographers exploded flashbulbs around him, and he smiled and talked about the four home runs when anybody asked him to comment.

"It's funny," he said at one point, "but I've never had any

unusual success here at Fenway Park. It's made for right-handed hitters, but I never did particularly well here."

"You did today!" shouted one of his mates.

Then Killebrew said something that labeled him again as a man more interested in the team's achievements than in his own.

"You know, it's fine to hit homers, but it's RBI's that mean the most. I'm happy I raised my runs batted in to ninety-five."

The next day Harmon hit his forty-fifth homer of the season, making it seven in the last six games. He hit no more the rest of the season, but the forty-five homers gave him the home run title for the second consecutive year.

In addition to this achievement, Harmon led the Twins in runs batted in with 96, total bases with 286, and slugging percentage with .555. The slugging percentage was also high enough to lead the league in this department.

And he had done it all with a twisted knee that had bothered him all season long, and despite the fact that he had missed twenty games!

14

Although Killebrew could not help being satisfied with his own performance in 1963, he was far from satisfied with the Twins' third-place finish. They had dropped a slot in the standings and had finished a big thirteen games behind the pennant-winning New York Yankees. Harmon went home to Ontario, Oregon, determined to have an operation on his knee, hoping that in 1964 he could have an even better year and help the Twins improve their standing in the American League race.

While Killebrew was home that fall two dramatic things happened—one in his personal life and one in the national life. In October, less than a month from the end of the season, Elaine presented Harmon with his fourth child—a girl whom the couple named Kathryn. Then, in November, Killebrew's happiness was dulled by a national tragedy when President John F. Kennedy was assassinated in Dallas, Texas. It was a sickening event that sorrowed the Killebrew family as it did all others.

Shortly after, on December 12, 1963, Harmon entered a hospital in Caldwell, Idaho, and underwent surgery. Dr. Donald Baranco, orthopedic physician, repaired some ruptured ligaments and removed cartilege, calcium and bone fragments from his injured knee, and Killebrew went through a period of painful recovery at the hospital and a later convalescence at home. Much to his delight, the knee gradually improved as the winter months passed, and as the time neared for spring training Killbrew was convinced that he would again be in top form for the coming season.

But the hope proved premature. Killebrew got away to a slow start in spring training. Before long it became evident that his knee was not entirely healed. He discovered he had to be careful when he ran and favor it when he was at bat. He found he was unable to work every day, and Mele was agreeable to letting Killebrew set his own pace. It meant that he missed some of the spring games entirely, and played four or five innings in others—and his hitting consequently suffered.

The Twins opened the regular season with substantially the same lineup as in 1963, with an exception which was to prove a major one—Tony Oliva, the Cuban outfielder destined to win the batting championship, was installed in right field.

In the first few weeks of the 1964 season the Twins stumbled badly. No one in the lineup was hitting particularly well, and the team played only .500 ball as they dawdled in the second division. The power they were expected to have failed to materialize.

There was one occasion, on May 3, when the Twins showed some of the power they were noted for, and the hopes of the fans soared. This was the day they went into the eleventh inning of a game with Kansas City, tied at 3–3, and broke up the ball game by tying a major league record.

Rookie Tony Oliva opened the eleventh inning against the Athletics' pitcher, Dan Pfister, by hitting a home run. Bob Allison followed by rapping one over the left field fence. Jim

Hall then duplicated Allison's homer with one into right field.

Stunned by three successive home runs, Pfister headed for the showers and reliefer Vern Handrahan came in. Killebrew, not to be outdone by his teammates, greeted him with a home run over the left field fence, his second of the game. The four successive home runs tied a major league record shared by the Cleveland Indians and the Milwaukee Braves.

But that was a rare display of power hitting, for the Twins were not exhibiting anything like this in their other games. Along with others, Killebrew's bat was strangely silent. He simply couldn't seem to get started. Even when he tagged the ball hard it seemed to go directly to a waiting outfielder. But more often than not he failed to get good wood on the ball. He knew that part of the trouble was his knee, for he still favored it some. But he also knew that every day the knee was getting stronger—and this excuse wasn't going to hold water for long!

During his slump Killebrew went to Ossie Bluege, the man who had signed him so long ago. Bluege was now serving the Twins as secretary and controller, and he and Harmon had continued a close relationship throughout the years.

"I thought maybe you could help me," Harmon said. "Nothing seems to go safe. My timing is off. I'm trying to figure if I'm doing something wrong."

Bluege looked at his protégé shrewdly. He knew all about slumps. He had been a third baseman for the old Washington Senators and had suffered through many of them.

"Don't worry about it, Harm," he said. "You'll get straightened out."

"Maybe so. But I'm going through a tough period. I know my knee isn't quite right yet, but I can't blame it all on that."

"You didn't get in all your training because of the knee,

you know," Bluege pointed out. "This held back your progress a little."

But Harmon wasn't satisfied. "I must be doing something wrong up there. Maybe I'm standing wrong, or something is wrong with my swing, or—"

"Look," said Bluege sharply. "You're a good hitter. Everybody knows what you can do. So don't let it get you down. I've been through a lot of slumps, and I've seen others go through them, and I've learned one thing—there isn't an awful lot you can do except let them run their course, like scarlet fever. Forget about where you're standing or how you're swinging. You're not doing anything wrong out there, Harm—you just haven't got your timing yet. A little extra batting practice, maybe, to get that back, and you'll be booming them out of here again."

But the slump continued to prey on Harmon's mind. He felt that he was not contributing as much to the team as he should be, and on May 9 he walked up to Mele in the clubhouse.

"Sam," he said, "I want to apologize for not doing better this year. I feel pretty bad about it."

Mele was caught off-guard momentarily, for seldom had a ballplayer come to him in such a contrite way.

"Harm, you don't have to apologize for anything," he said finally. "Everybody knows they'll start falling in for you. How's the knee?"

"Well, it feels stronger every day."

"I'll tell you what I'm going to do," Mele said. "I'm going to rest you a few days—you and your knee. Maybe that will snap you out of it."

"If you think so," said Killebrew, "it's okay with me. But I'd like to take a little extra batting practice, if I could."

"We'll see to it," said Mele.

A few minutes later Mele was talking to a sportswriter. He

was still shaking his head over the fact that Killebrew had come to him with an apology.

"Harmon's a great guy," he said, "an absolutely great guy. Nobody tries harder than he does. He'll break his slump, there's no doubt about that. And to think the guy came up and wanted to apologize—"

On that day Killebrew and his anemic .167 batting average were removed from the game. Jim Hall took his place in left field. For four days Harmon fretted on the bench, but he took his extra batting practice and he did very well, too. He clouted several long drives over the fence in left field, and he hit a lot of "singles and doubles" squarely on the nose.

On May 14, with the Twins trailing the White Sox, Yankees, Indians and Orioles in the standings, Mele put Killebrew back in left field and benched Hall.

Killebrew was on the spot. If he delivered it could be the turning point of the year for him; if he failed to come through it could mean a long dismal season.

The Twins met the Chicago White Sox at home that day and Chicago started rookie Gary Peters on the mound. In the opening inning the first two Twins were easy outs. Then the fireworks started. Rich Rollins sent a screaming double into left center. Bob Allison walked. Killebrew was up for the first time in five days, and the thought went through his mind, *Will I have my timing back now?*

He stepped gingerly into the batter's box and dug a hole with his right toe. Peters, although a rookie, had plenty of guts. He fired a fast ball past Killebrew as if the feared slugger weren't even there. Then, just to show his contempt, he broke a curve over the outside edge of the plate for strike two. Killebrew had been fooled by both pitches and had not yet taken the bat off his shoulder.

Peters went into a short stretch, glanced at the base runners, and fired another fast one. This time Harmon swung.

The sharp *crack* could be heard all over the stadium, and the ball soared high into the left field stands for his fifth homer of the year!

As Killebrew returned to the dugout after rounding the bases, his teammates almost fought for a chance to slap him on the back.

"Maybe that rest did you some good," said Mele.

"I hope so," replied Killebrew with a broad grin. "That one sure felt good when I hit it."

For the rest of the game the Twins, responding to Killebrew's return to the lineup, went on a home run rampage. In the third Zoilo Versalles and Don Mincher both hit homers. In the fourth Rich Rollins and Bob Allison hit circuit clouts.

Then, in the eighth, Killebrew came up to face the crafty reliefer Don Mossi. He swung at the first pitch and blasted his second home run of the game into the left field seats!

A great roar came from the fans and poured down on Killebrew like a warm shower. He went back to the dugout and sat down on the bench, feeling suddenly much better than he had felt all season.

"I think I'll keep you in the lineup," was Mele's understatement of the day.

The Twins coasted to a 15–7 victory on their six home runs.

"Boy!" said a writer to Killebrew after the game. "You must have come back in there today to catch up on your homers!"

But Killebrew shook his head. "No, I didn't really. I didn't have any thought about coming back to hit home runs." Then he grinned sheepishly. "But I'll say they didn't hurt my feelings any, either."

Later in May the Twins moved to New York for a series with the Yankees. The evening before the opening game

Killebrew and Allison sat in their room at the Roosevelt Hotel and watched television. Suddenly there was a knock on the door. Killebrew got up and answered. It was Mele.

"Harm," the manager said, "I just got word that there's a kid over in New York Hospital who's recovering from some burns he got as an altar boy in church. His robe caught fire as he was lighting some candles, and he received first-degree burns over fifty per cent of his body. He's been in the hospital about three weeks, and he's recovering now and can have visitors. The reason I'm mentioning this to you, Harm— well, you happen to be his favorite ballplayer."

Without hesitation, Harmon said, "I'll go see the boy before the game tomorrow. What's his name?"

"John Guiney."

"I'll look him up."

The next morning when Killebrew walked into the room, the boy's eyes almost popped out of his head.

"You're—you're Harmon Killebrew!" he exclaimed.

"Yes. You're John Guiney, aren't you?"

"Yes. Yes, sir."

Killebrew sat down at the boy's bedside.

"How old are you, John?"

"Eight."

Killebrew smiled. "That's a real coincidence. I have a boy and he's eight too."

The boy said nothing, a little speechless at having his idol sitting by his bedside. Killebrew took an autographed ball from his pocket.

"Would you like to have it, John?" he asked.

"Boy! Would I!"

The young boy made frantic motions beneath his pillow and finally pulled out a worn baseball glove.

"Would you autograph my glove too?" he asked eagerly.

"I sure will." Harmon took out a pen and carefully signed his name on the glove.

"Do you play baseball, John?" he asked.

"You bet! I'm a shortstop."

"That's another coincidence. I used to be a shortstop in high school and the sandlots, but not very much in the big leagues. Where do you play ball, John?"

"Over in Prospect Park," said the boy.

"I'll tell you what," Killebrew said. "You hurry up and get well, and the next time we're in town you can come out to the ball park and meet all the fellows."

"Gee, that'd be swell!" Young John's eyes sparkled with anticipation. "I'm going to watch you play on TV today. The doctors said I could."

"Good," said Killebrew. "Maybe I'll hit you a couple."

When Harmon left the hospital he wondered a little at his rashness in making such a statement. You didn't hit home runs just because you wanted to—the opposing pitcher always had something to say about it. He knew he was out on the limb. He was not given to making such predictions, but sympathy for the boy had brought the words to his lips—and it would be a shame, now, if he didn't make good.

The Yankees, fighting as usual for the pennant, started Ralph Terry against the Twins. But in the very first inning the Twins treated him like a cousin. Versalles opened with a single to center. Rollins then hammered a triple over Mickey Mantle's head to bring Versalles home. Then rookie Tony Oliva, who was showing marked signs of being a tremendous hitter, banged one into the Yankee bullpen in right field for a home run to score behind Rollins.

Bob Allison kept up the bombardment by slamming a double into left center. Hall struck out to bring up Killebrew with Allison on second and one away. After a little mental debate, Yankee manager Yogi Berra decided to let Terry pitch to one more batter, and that proved a mistake. Killebrew hit one into the left field seats for a home run that completed a five-run inning.

As he circled the bases, Killebrew grinned to himself. *Well, he thought, at least I hit one for the kid!*

And in the clinical-white room of New York Hospital, a smile broke across the face of John Guiney.

In the eighth inning Harmon came to bat again, this time with the bases empty and against reliefer Steve Hamilton. And when Hamilton placed one on the outside corner, Killebrew drove it high and far into the right center seats for his second homer of the day!

Later, in the dugout, he said to Allison, "Bob, I don't know what in the world ever induced me to tell that boy I'd maybe hit a couple for him. But I'm sure glad I did. I feel good all over!"

It was almost incidental that the Twins defeated the Yanks, 7–4.

Killebrew's bombardment of American League pitching continued until the end of May. From May 14, when he returned to the lineup with his .167 batting average, until May 30, Harmon hit ten home runs in 16 days and increased his batting average to .257.

But the Twins faltered in June. By the middle of the month they were still in fifth place, but now seven games behind league-leading Chicago. The team was playing badly. Their hitting had tailed off. They were in an unexplainable slump.

Desperate, the Twins' top management decided drastic measures were necessary to yank the team out of the doldrums. On June 11 everyone on the club was shaken by word that the Twins had traded Vic Power and outfielder Len

Green to the Los Angeles Angels for infielder Jerry Kindall and infielder-outfielder Frank Kostro.

"We think this trade will help us," said Mele, "but our real need is still a good right-handed pitcher."

On June 16 the Twins obtained the right-handed pitcher they had been wanting. They sent pitcher Lee Stange to the Cleveland Indians and obtained Jim (Mudcat) Grant in exchange.

"That's what we needed," said Mele. "I think Grant will be a big help to us."

But the Twins continued to slip. On June 20 they played a particularly bad game against the Tigers at Bloomington. For some time they had been playing indifferent baseball, making mental rather than mechanical errors—throwing to the wrong base, failing to hit the cutoff man on throws from the outfield, the pitcher failing to cover first on a ground ball to the right side. Mele finally blew his top.

"We're playing lax baseball," he said. "Those that don't play heads-up from now on will be fined. I'm going to be sole judge on misplays, and the fines will be more than fifty dollars."

However, there was one ray of light in the Twins' sad game against the Tigers, which they lost 8–7. Tiger manager Charlie Dressen decided to challenge Killebrew with an infield shift. Since Harmon was primarily a pull hitter, driving the ball into center or left field, Dressen had his infield shift dramatically to the left. Third baseman Don Wert played a deep third, shortstop Dick McAuliffe swung into the "hole" between third and short, and second baseman Jerry Lumpe played on the third base side of second base! They were going to stop anything Killebrew hit toward left if they possibly could!

So Killebrew crossed them up. With plenty of real estate

between first and second base, he calmly drilled a single into *right* field. The next time he hit to right too, only this one was so far out of reach that no infield could have taken it. It landed in the right field seats!

"Didn't do us much good, did it?" Dressen admitted afterward.

"The trouble with that Killebrew," said one Tiger player, "is that he can hit to right just about as hard as he hits to left. The guy's got so much power he can knock 'em out of the lot when he's tryin' to hold back on his swing!"

About this time three Twin players were chosen on the All-Star team. They were Killebrew, left field; Allison, first base; and Oliva, right field.

It was Killebrew's fourth year on the All-Star team. "I think," he said, "that it means more to be chosen on the team by your fellow players. It's quite an honor."

A week later the Twins met the Chicago White Sox in a close pitchers' battle. The score was Chicago 3, Twins 2 in the seventh inning, and knuckle-ball artist Hoyt Wilhelm was baffling the Minnesota Twins as he held on to the precarious lead. With one out in the seventh, Wilhelm let a couple of knuckle balls get away from him and walked Tony Oliva. It was Harmon's turn to bat, and he went up there wondering if he could connect squarely with Wilhelm's fluttery pitches.

He expected a knuckler on the first pitch, and he got it. The ball danced over the plate like something alive and Harmon swung. The ball soared high and far into the left field seats—foul!

The next pitch was a knuckler outside, followed by another inside. Ball two, strike one.

The fourth pitch was another knuckler, jumping crazily, and Killebrew fouled it into the stands. With a two-and-two count, Wilhelm served him still another knuckler. Killebrew swung and topped the squirmy pitch, foul.

Killebrew stepped back and knocked dirt out of his spiked shoes as he tried to collect his poise. Wilhelm's knuckler was alive. It was hopping, sailing, jumping and taking off. There was no telling which way it would break. It was an almost impossible pitch to hit squarely.

Wilhelm took his stretch, hesitated, then delivered the ball again—another butterfly pitch. Killebrew swung and this time caught the elusive ball on the nose. It rose majestically and disappeared over the left field fence for his twenty-sixth home run, putting the Twins ahead. Allison then hit another homer to make the final score Twins 5, Chicago 3.

By July 5 the Twins were in fourth place and were playing only .500 ball. But on that day Killebrew hit his thirtieth home run plus three singles to help beat the Yankees at New York by a 9–2 count. It was a signal for still more speculation.

The season was at its halfway mark; Killebrew was halfway to sixty homers. Sportswriters crowded around to hear what Harmon would say now about beating the home run record. He was noncommittal.

"You have to stay hot to do it," he said. "It's no cinch."

"Do you think you can do it?"

"I don't know if I can stay hot," he replied. "I'm streaky."

One disgruntled writer was dissatisfied with the answer. He grumbled to another reporter, "Why doesn't Killebrew come out and say yes or no, he will or he won't?"

"Because he's too smart to answer that way," was the answer. "He doesn't want to jinx himself by saying he won't, and he's too modest to say he will. And besides, it's an unanswerable question—no one knows if he can do it, including himself."

The season halted temporarily while the Nationals won the All-Star Game, 7–4. After the break the teams resumed the pennant race, and the Twins immediately began to fade.

Stumbling and reeling, they lost eleven out of twelve games and fell into sixth place.

During this depressing time Killebrew showed his true value to the team. Mele noticed it and so did the players. He continued hitting well as the rest of the team collapsed. He began making sensational diving catches in left field—something he was not exactly noted for—and he tried desperately to snap the other players out of the doldrums by his example on the field and his talk in the dugout.

"It looks as though you're trying to spark this club," a writer said to him one day. "Are you, Harm?"

Killebrew shrugged. "I don't know how to answer you," he said. "Every player tries his best every game. I'm trying to end this slump the best way I can, by fielding or hitting or anything—but so are all the other guys."

An example of Killebrew's inspirational play occurred on July 31 when the Twins met the Yanks at Metropolitan Stadium, although he didn't start out in promising fashion. Killebrew struck out twice against Al Downing with men waiting to be driven in, and partly because of his failure to produce with runners on, the Twins were trailing the Yankess, 3–2, when they came to bat in the last of the ninth.

Downing, pitching a steady game, got the first man in the ninth, and it began to look like a lost cause for the Twins. Rollins kept a glimmering of hope alive when he singled to right, but this hope faded again when Oliva flied to left for the second out. Two gone and a runner on first.

Mele paced back and forth in the dugout, then came to a stop as Killebrew stepped up to the plate and dug in. Downing took his time, then brushed Harmon back with the first pitch. Killebrew took a little walk around the plate and dug in again. The next pitch was knee-high and over the plate for a strike.

As soon as the umpire's hand went up, a loud fan in the park let go with a blast.

"Old Harmless Harm! Strike 'im out, Downing, and end the agony!"

But "Harmless Harm" had other ideas. He connected with Downing's next pitch and rode it into the stands for a two-run homer that won the game, 4–3.

In the clubhouse afterward, he was being congratulated by his teammates, but Harmon wasn't as concerned about his personal success as he was about the affect the close victory would have on the team.

"We needed a win like that, one that we pulled out of the fire," he said. "The way we've been going, that homer meant more to me than any other I can remember. I hope it gets us rolling again."

It really didn't, though, because the Twins finished in sixth place. However, Killebrew ended the season with forty-nine home runs—the highest total of his career and enough to win the home run crown for the third year in a row.

That feat put him in a select class. Only three American League players and four National League players had ever led their leagues in home runs for three or more consecutive years.

Ralph Kiner, of the Pittsburgh Pirates, holds the all-time record of seven straight years, although in two of those years he tied with Johnny Mize of New York and in one year with Hank Sauer of Chicago. Babe Ruth had two streaks, four in a row from 1918 to 1921, and six in a row from 1926 to 1931. The other streaks hardly count, for they were back in the dead-ball days when ten homers a season was a mighty feat indeed.

During the winter more honors came to Harmon. He was called from his home in Oregon to attend the Tops-in-Sports

Banquet in Baltimore, Maryland, in December. Here he was saluted as the 1964 Sultan of Swat. A crown of jewels was presented, emblematic of the major league home run championship. Previous winners had been Mickey Mantle, Ted Williams, Ernie Banks, Eddie Mathews, Hank Aaron, Willie Mays and Roger Maris.

15

~~~~~~

Despite a sixth-place finish in 1964—twenty full games behind the pennant-winning Yankees—Sam Mele was given a
new contract to manage the Twins shortly after the season
ended. At about the same time Billy Martin, formerly a
Yankee and Twin player, was signed to a coaching contract.
In announcing these maneuvers, Cal Griffith said, "Our team
last season suffered the worst collapse of a potentially promising team in American League history. Billy Martin is explo-
sive, and we expect him to build a fire under the Twins in
1965."

One other addition to the coaching staff particularly delighted Harmon—Jim Lemon was brought back as a batting
coach.

After the 1964 season Killebrew, Bob Allison, Earl Battey
and Bill Dailey went to Alaska to hold some baseball clinics
for young boys. They were greeted by Suzy Marlin (Miss
Alaska) and visited both Fairbanks and Anchorage. In addition to holding the clinics, the players were introduced to
baseball Alaskan-style—on snowshoes!

But for the most part Harmon stayed home with his growing family and enjoyed their company as much as he could
before reporting again for spring training.

Killebrew had no difficulty coming to terms with Griffith on his 1965 contract. He signed for $50,000 to become the first player in the history of the club to receive that much. Then he went south determined to relearn the art of playing at first base again—because rumors had it that he was to be switched back to the infield.

"I'll have a lot of work to do," he said. "It's tougher returning to first base from the outfield than it is going from first base to the outfield. You're in practically every play in the infield and it makes a difference."

When the players assembled at Tinker Field in Orlando, they found themselves playing on Minnesota soil. The field at Tinker had been bad, with soft spots and pebbles. It had been on one of those soft spots that Killebrew had wrenched his knee in 1963, and Earl Battey had experienced similar injuries on a number of occasions. To rectify the situation, the entire field had been resurfaced with soil shipped down from Minnesota.

"It took three hundred and fifty cubic yards at two thousand and thirty pounds per cubic yard," said Griffith. "It's the same dirt we have on our infield at Metropolitan Stadium."

"It'll be just like playing at home," cracked one of the players.

It was a vast improvement in the field, but it didn't seem to improve the performance of the team. The Twins looked sluggish through the early days of training, and their appearance didn't encourage anyone to predict much of a season for them.

But Killebrew's shift to first base was not one of the Twins' problems. Harmon responded beautifully to the challenge. He relearned the position rapidly. In the first few days he made several good stops on badly thrown balls, and once made a diving stab of a line drive that was unbelievable.

"Good," said Mele. "He reacts like an infielder. He'll be all right."

One thing that helped Harmon was that his knee was now in excellent shape, and he could make the quick turns and stops required of an infielder.

But the Twins, in general, were lifeless during the exhibition games. No one was hitting, the pitching was only fair, and the fielding was atrocious. They lost games with alarming consistency. Martin kept promising that when the season started the Twins would snap out of it, but apparently Griffith was not convinced.

"I'd like to see a little more spirit down here, too," he snapped.

Besides the limp play, there were nasty rumors hurting the club. Some people said that Billy Martin was after Mele's job, but Martin denied it vehemently. There was an open clash between Mele and Versalles, and the shortstop was fined three hundred dollars. The rumors of dissension on the club were at their height as the team finally quit its Florida base and moved north for their opener with the New York Yankees at Bloomington.

The state of Minnesota had just survived one of its worst winters, and a week before the opening game there was still snow and ice on the field. As the opener neared, the condition of the weather in this far-north big league city became something of a joke. Just before the season got under way, Griffith received a tongue-in-cheek telegram from A. E. Hagberg, president of the Greater Fairbanks Chamber of Commerce in Alaska. It said:

"Fairbanks enjoying spring baseball weather as final traces of winter snow disappears. Near 50-above temperatures during past week, plus spring appearance of our midnight sun, present inviting prospect for opening Minnesota Twins' season in Fairbanks if mid-winter Alaskan weather prevails in

Twin Cities. Please advise if we may assist you in making Fairbanks baseball facilities available for opening of season."

Despite all the joking, however, the weather did moderate just before the opening game.

After posting an 11–15 record in the Grapefruit League, the Twins got off on the right foot in their opener by beating the Yankees in an eleven-inning game, 5–4. As April progressed the Twins established themselves as at least an early pennant threat. Doing a complete about-face, they battled the Chicago White Sox for first place right from the opening date, with first one team holding a slight edge, then the other.

Killebrew swung a red-hot bat from the very beginning. By the end of April he was hitting .333, but he had failed to get a home run. Instead, he was hitting the ball straight away— line drives that went for singles and doubles. At the same time, Tony Oliva seemed to be hitting the homers for the team, at one point getting three in two days. In the clubhouse one day Killebrew grinned at Oliva.

"All right, Tony," he said. "You hit the homers and I'll go for the singles."

Mele heard the exchange. "That's all right with me, as long as we keep winning," he commented.

No one really seemed worried that Killebrew was not connecting for the long ball—least of all Harmon, himself. In the last four years he had hit 46, 48, 45 and 49 homers, leading the league the last three seasons, and no one doubted that he would come up with a presentable figure in 1965.

"I'm just not getting everything into my swing yet," he said on April 30.

The home runs started to come on May 2 in an important doubleheader with the first-place White Sox. The Twins were close on the heels of the Sox and needed a victory badly.

The day before the twin bill, Killebrew took some extra batting practice, mainly to get his timing oriented. That night he received wonderful news from home—his wife had given birth to a new baby daughter, Erin. A happy Harmon Killebrew faced the White Sox the next day.

Chicago jumped off to a one-run lead in the first inning off Jim Kaat, and this 1–0 lead held for six agonizing innings. During this time Killebrew got a single, but it was wasted.

In the last of the seventh Chicago increased its lead to 2–0. But in the top of the eighth the Twins came alive. Rich Rollins was on first base as a result of a single when Killebrew came to bat. Hoyt Wilhelm, the tough knuckle-baller, was pitching for the White Sox.

Wilhelm threw nothing but his flutterball to Harmon, but he made the mistake of getting one over the center of the plate. Killebrew drove it over the 425-foot center field fence to tie the score at 2–2.

It was his first home run of the 1965 season.

The tie endured until the tenth inning. Zoilo Versalles was first man up to greet reliefer Bob Locker. He rapped a hot shot through the box and into center for a single. Rollins then laid down a perfect sacrifice bunt to move Versalles to second. This brought up Killebrew.

Locker got a quick first strike over on Harmon, then fed him one on the outside for a ball. The third pitch was a curve that cut the corner for strike two.

Killebrew waggled his bat, then cocked it over his shoulder as Locker took his stretch. It was a fast ball on the inside corner and Harmon swung. The ball went like a shot down the third base line, past the third sacker and into left field to bring home Versalles with the winning run.

Killebrew not only had connected for his first round-tripper, but had driven in all three runs in the Twins' 3–2 victory.

Unfortunately for the Twins' cause, the White Sox grabbed

the second game, 5–4, and stayed at the top of the standings with a 10–5 record as against the Twins' 9–5.

In the clubhouse Killebrew, who also got a hit in the second contest, was all smiles.

"That first homer felt good," he said. "Let's say I hit it for my new baby daughter."

The next day was an off-day and Harmon flew home to Ontario, Orgeon, to visit his wife and his fifth child. He was back in Twin Cities in time for the next game.

On May 10 the Twins edged the White Sox in a tight game, 4–3, and grabbed first place.

On the first of June they were still on top, but with only a half-game lead over the pursuing Chicago White Sox. These two teams traded first place back and forth as the month of June progressed, with Detroit, Cleveland and Baltimore breathing down their necks.

During this tense month Harmon accomplished another thing that was to mean a great deal to the Twins in their drive for the pennant. Mele noticed it and so did the other players. In his own quiet way, and by his example on the field, Killebrew was becoming the acknowledged team leader. Harmon's presence in the lineup gave the team more confidence, and inspired others to do more than their best. The result was one of the great team efforts of all time, with each player unselfishly minimizing his own importance and playing for the good of the team.

Killebrew, himself, set the prime example when in mid-June the Twins were playing in Detroit. Tiger Stadium has a short "front porch" in right field, an inviting target for left-handed hitters. On the Twins' bench was Don Mincher, an able first baseman with a potent bat. Killebrew knew that Mele longed to get Mincher's bat in the lineup. But there seemed no chance as long as Harmon held down the initial sack.

Finally Killebrew went to Mele. "Sam," he said, "if you want to get Mincher in there against right-handed pitchers or something, I'll be glad to switch to third base."

"Thanks, Harm," said Mele gratefully. "I'll think that one over."

A few days later second baseman Jerry Kindall was injured and Mele shifted Rich Rollins to second, put Killebrew at third, and installed Mincher at first.

Killebrew's unselfish example was typical of the Twins' team spirit. Jim Grant, who hated to start games and relieve too, nevertheless volunteered to do so. And toward the end of June, when the Twins were beset by one injury after another, either the substitutes came up with chips-down performances or the hurt player played over his injury. Jim Kaat, despite tendonitis in his arm, missed only one turn. Versalles played with two leg bruises, a pulled groin muscle and a sore foot. Oliva played with two badly swollen knees. Early Battey was knocked out of the lineup seven times with injuries but bounced right back. Jim Hall suffered a knee injury. Bob Allison fractured his wrist. Jerry Kindall was out two weeks with a bad hip. Pitcher Dave Boswell was floored by mononucleosis. Jim Grant pitched despite trouble with his knees. And Camilo Pascual missed games repeatedly with a pulled back muscle.

In one stretch of games Mele had to use eight different infield lineups in eight days. And he had to start relief pitchers instead of regulars in game after game—but they delivered.

Despite their unbelievable string of injuries, the Twins had a three-and-a-half-game lead over Cleveland by the All-Star break. Baltimore was four and a half behind in third, with Chicago and Detroit trailing by six and seven games. In the All-Star Game, which was played for the first time in the Twins' Metropolitan Stadium, six Minnesota players appeared—Killebrew, Hall, Battey, Grant, Versalles and Oliva.

Killebrew, appearing for his seventh time, contributed a home run to the American League cause, but the Nationals won, 6–5.

While the Twins were enjoying their first-place position in the standings, the perennial pennant-winning New York Yankees were in the doldrums, thirteen and a half games behind in sixth place. It was a critical moment for the Yanks, who still entertained hopes of fighting their way to the top, when on July 12 they clashed with the Twins in a memorable game at Bloomington.

There were 35,263 fans in the stands when Twins pitcher Jim Kaat faced the first Yankee batter. The Bombers started out as if they owned Kaat by greeting him with four hits for one run in the initial frame. But in the bottom of the third Versalles hit a bases-empty homer off Yankee starter Al Downing to knot the score at 1-all. Then, in the fourth, the Twins surged ahead on singles by Oliva, Killebrew and Battey, plus a sacrifice fly by Hall. That made the score 3–1.

In the top of the fifth the Yankees knocked Kaat out of the game with a two-run attack that tied the score a 3–3. But the Twins scored again in the last half of the fifth when the speedy Versalles came all the way home from first base on Rollins' double to left. The Twins were now ahead, 4–3.

In the top of the seventh the Yankees knotted the score again at 4–4 when Twin reliefer Bill Pleis wild-pitched Elston Howard home with the tying marker.

The ninth inning was packed with excitement. In the Yankee half Howard led off with a single off Twin relief pitcher Jerry Fosnow. Hector Lopez lined out, but Joe Pepitone was safe on an error by Rollins. Clete Boyer flied to right and Howard went to third after the catch. Runners on first and third and two out.

Roger Repoz topped a bouncer down the first base line. Fosnow came off the mound, scooped up the ball and tagged

Repoz as he went by—then dropped the ball. First base umpire John Flaherty called Repoz safe, but home plate umpire Ed Hurley ruled him out, claiming Repoz interfered with Fosnow as he fielded the ball. Meantime, Howard came racing home from third.

There was the usual argument, and after a consultation between Hurley and Flaherty, Repoz was again called safe. Sam Mele then exploded off the Twins' bench, and when he couldn't change the umpire's mind, he continued the game under protest.

The score was now Yankees 5, Twins 4, with the last of the ninth coming up. The Yankees' Pete Mikkelsen was now pitching, and when he got Versalles on a soft fly, things looked bad for the Twins. Rollins walked, but Oliva was another easy out. Man on first, two out, Killebrew at bat.

Harmon already had two hits in three times up, and Mikkelsen took great care in pitching to the husky slugger. A curve caught the outside corner for strike one. The next two pitches were low for balls. Killebrew swung and fouled one off. A pitch was in too tight. The count had gone to three-and two.

It was a dramatic situation. One run behind, a man on first, two outs in the ninth inning, and a three-and-two count. The Yankees were a possible one pitch away from victory.

Mikkelsen, owner of a sinking fast ball, tried to get it by Killebrew around the knees. But the pitch came in too high, dipped a little, and cut the plate belt-high. Harmon swung. The ball took off on a line and slammed into the left field stands for a game-winning home run! Twins 6, Yanks 5!

The homer was only the sixteenth of the year for Killebrew, but it was one of the most satisfying he had ever hit. It provided a five-game hold on first place for the Twins, and it was felt by most baseball observers that the Twins' victory was the last straw for the sinking Yankees—the one game that could be pointed to afterward as the coup de grace.

The Twins, with the spirit that had dominated the team from the beginning, yelled and waved towels as Harmon circled the bases. They mauled him affectionately as he entered the dugout. But Harmon got the best compliment of all when he walked into the clubhouse after the game. His seven-year-old son, Kenny, was on hand to greet him.

"That was a nice home run you hit, Daddy," he said.

Killebrew talked modestly to reporters as he munched on a piece of watermelon near his locker. A reporter asked him how it felt to beat the Yankees in the ninth on a homer.

"It felt good," admitted Harmon. "That homer was one of the sweeter of the sweet."

During July the Twins continued their winning ways, and by the end of that month they still retained a five-game lead over Baltimore and Cleveland, who were tied for second place. It was an amazing performance, considering the rash of injuries the club had suffered.

Then came the black day of August 2.

The Twins were hosts to the Baltimore Orioles that day in Metropolitan Stadium at Bloomington. In the third inning the Twins grabbed a 2–0 lead and were still hanging on grimly when the top of the sixth opened for the Orioles. But Baltimore's Luis Aparicio led off the inning with a homer, and the score was 2–1. The next Baltimore hitter was center fielder Russ Snyder. Snyder topped a pitch from Jim Merritt and dribbled it down the third base line. Rich Rollins raced in, grabbed the slow hopper and winged it to Killebrew at first. The throw was to the home plate side of first base and Killebrew reached out his left arm to take the throw as Snyder thundered toward him. Ball and runner arrived at the same time, and Snyder, coming into the bag, smashed into Killebrew's outstretched arm.

The sickening thud could be heard all over the stadium. The ball went into short right field, and Snyder, unhurt, raced to second. But Killebrew, with fiery pain shooting through his left arm, writhed on the ground!

Through the dim haze of pain Killebrew saw a forest of legs and arms approaching him as players converged on the scene. He felt hands on him and the soft voice of Dr. Bill Proffitt, but for a few minutes he knew nothing but the blinding pain that raced through his arm and shoulder.

Meantime, a deathly silence gripped the spectators. They knew what this could mean. If Killebrew was hurt, along with all the other injuries the team had suffered, it could well end the Twins' bid for the pennant. They watched anxiously as the players of both teams gathered around the fallen Killebrew, and when they saw the prostrate form on the ground lifted to a stretcher and gently carried off, a low groan of misery escaped the fans.

This, surely, looked like the final blow.

In the clubhouse Dr. Proffitt saw at once that Killebrew had suffered a complete dislocation of the elbow. While Harmon gritted his teeth, he pulled the elbow back in place. Later, X-rays were taken. They showed no fracture.

"He should be back in the lineup in two weeks," said the doctor optimistically.

That night was a sleepless one for Harmon as pain continued to torment him. By the next day the elbow was swollen to twice its normal size, but Dr. Proffitt was sure Killebrew would return to the lineup in two weeks.

Killebrew was not so sure. "The left arm is my swinging arm with the bat; the right arm only guides the bat," he said. "We'll have to wait and see."

Manager Mele shook his head sadly. He had received additional bad news on that same black day of August 2. He was told that Camilo Pascual, operated on for torn muscles in his back, would not be back for a month—and perhaps not for the rest of the season.

The seriousness of the Twins' plight could be seen in the records of the two players. Pascual had posted an 8–3 record despite persistent arm trouble. Killebrew, when hurt, was leading the league in RBI's with 70, was tied for the lead in home runs with 22, was hitting .280, and was batting .378 with runners on second and third base.

"This team," said Mele, "has suffered more injuries than any club in baseball history. But everybody tries harder and keeps fighting back. It's the best team effort I've ever seen."

The day after Killebrew's injury Mele gave a rare pep talk to his team. "We're just going to have to try harder with Harmon out," he said. "This hasn't been a one-man show up to now, although Harmon certainly has been the leader. There's no reason why we can't continue to win."

As Bob Fowler, *Minneapolis Tribune* writer, put it, "It was a tough talk to make. It was King Arthur telling his knights to go into battle without Sir Lancelot."

The Twins posted a motto on the bulletin board: "A hero a day keeps the contenders away"—and this was the manner in which they continued to win. Every day a different player would deliver the key hit or make the game-saving fielding play. Remarkably, in the next week they actually increased their league lead to eight and a half games.

Killebrew was permitted to go home to Ontario, Oregon, for a short time, but during most of his recovery period he sat on the Minnesota bench. Mele felt that Harmon's presence, in itself, was an inspiration to the rest of the team.

But, despite optimistic predictions, Killebrew's elbow was slower to heal than had first been thought. All of August slipped by, and by Labor Day Harmon was still unable to stretch his arm to full length or to bend it normally.

Sitting idly on the bench as his team battled for a pennant

was as agonizing to Harmon as the injury itself. In close games particularly, where his own bat might have made a difference, Harmon felt a frustration that was almost unbearable. But he helped keep the other players in a winning frame of mind by his comments and encouragement on the bench.

"One of the quietest team leaders of all time," remarked a sportswriter, "but a leader nevertheless."

About mid-September Killebrew began taking batting practice regularly, and on September 23 he finally returned to the game—after seven frustrating weeks of idleness.

"I hope to play from now until the end of the season," he said, "and get my timing back for the World Series."

Three days later, on September 26, the Minnesota Twins clinched their first American League pennant by whipping Baltimore, 2–1. On September 28, Killebrew hit his first home run since returning to the lineup. It was his twenty-third of the season.

Harmon hit two more before the season ended to raise his total to twenty-five, high for the club. He might well have won the league home run championship again had he not missed forty-eight games during his injury. Tony Conigliaro, of the Boston Red Sox, took the 1965 title with a modest thirty-two, only seven more than Killebrew hit.

Although Killebrew batted .269 and drove in seventy-five runs, his 1965 performance was overshadowed by the fact that the Twins captured the flag, Tony Oliva grabbed the batting championship for the second straight year, and Zoilo Versalles emerged as one of the finest shortstops in the league and was eventually voted the league's Most Valuable Player.

The World Series between the Minnesota Twins and the Los Angeles Dodgers was a bigger-than-usual thrill for Harmon Killebrew. Since his first big year in 1959, Harmon had played on teams that finished eighth on two occasions, seventh, second, third and sixth. For the first time in his career he was on a pennant winner, and he was at a loss for words when reporters probed for his reaction.

"I have a lot of thoughts, but I don't know how to express them," he said humbly. "I know playing on a pennant winner is something every ballplayer looks forward to. I'm no exception."

The Dodgers were 7–5 favorites to win the World Series when the two teams clashed in the first game at Metropolitan Stadium in Bloomington. It was felt that the Dodgers had too much pitching for the Twins, and that Don Drysdale and Sandy Koufax would prove to be unbeatable.

The experts received a severe jolt when the hit-happy Twins drove Drysdale from the box in the opener, defeating him 8–2, and then bombed Koufax on the second day to win 5–1. It was pretty heady stuff, and the Twins were in a soaring frame of mind as they flew to Los Angeles to meet the Dodgers in the third game at Chavez Ravine. But the Twins' booming bats were stilled by Claude Osteen and they were shut out, 4–0.

It was the beginning of disaster. In the next two games Drysdale and Koufax got their revenge, defeating the Twins 7–2 and 7–0—and the Twins went back home trailing by a game.

Jim (Mudcat) Grant staved off final defeat for the Twins by winning the sixth game, 5–1. But the Dodgers threw Koufax into the fray in the seventh and final game, and the superb hurler allowed the Twins only three hits and defeated them, 2–0.

The defeat in the Series was bitter, but the 1965 season had not been without its glories. The Twins had battled through a long and tough year and had won the pennant despite a list of injuries that would have stopped a lesser club, and they had stretched the World Series to the maximum seven games

before going down to defeat—and thus had posted their best
season since moving to Minnesota in 1961. In the Series, Killebrew, fresh off the bench from his disastrous injury, tied
Zoilo Versalles for the best batting average. Killebrew had
.286 on six hits in twenty-one at bats, including one home
run. Versalles had .286 on eight hits in twenty-eight times
at bat, also including a homer.

There is no doubt that Harmon Killebrew ranks as one of
the great right-handed sluggers of all time. At the age of
twenty-nine and with seven full seasons of big league play
behind him, Killebrew has hit 297 home runs, just three
short of the coveted 300 mark. He is sure to make that next
season, and barring severe injury, he will most likely reach
the 400 home run mark someday. That is a feat accomplished
by only ten players in major league history—Babe Ruth,
Jimmy Foxx, Ted Williams, Mel Ott, Lou Gehrig, Stan
Musial, Eddie Mathews, Ed Snider, Mickey Mantle and Willie Mays. The first four players named hit 500 or more homers—and that's another possible goal for Killebrew should he
be able to play another six or seven years.

But although hitting the long ball is Killebrew's forte, he
is more than just a slugger. By sheer determination he has
overcome his early fielding difficulties and has emerged as a
solid all-around ballplayer capable of holding down two infield positions and an outfield spot. And Mele recognizes him
as a genuine team leader whose presence in the lineup in-
spires the other players to do their best. Quiet and unassuming, Harmon would be the first one to deny his greatness. His
first interest is in the team, rather than in his own personal
accomplishments. And in a broader light, his interest is in
the game of baseball itself. On many occasions he has expressed his thanks to the game for everything it has done for
him and his family, and anything he can do to further the
game or satisfy his fans he will do without question.

Outside the town of Payette, Idaho, there is a sign that says, "Welcome to Payette—Home of Harmon Killebrew." A street has been named after him, and his No. 12 football jersey still hangs prominently in the hall of Payette High School. The town where he was born has not forgotten him— nor will baseball. There seems no doubt that someday, because of his tremendous contributions to the game, this small-town Idaho boy will see his name emblazoned in baseball's Hall of Fame in Cooperstown.

HARMON CLAYTON KILLEBREW

Born: June 29, 1936

Bats right, throws right
Outfielder—Infielder

Weight: 210 pounds
Height: 5'11"

Year	Club	G	AB	R	H	2B	3B	HR	RBI	BA	PO	A	E	FA
1954	Washington	9	13	1	4	1	0	0	3	.308	5	2	0	1.000
1955	Washington	38	80	12	16	1	0	4	7	.200	24	49	5	.936
1956	Charlotte	70	249	61	81	16	7	15	63	.325	62	127	14	.931
1956	Washington	44	99	10	22	2	0	5	13	.222	24	44	4	.944
1957	Chattanooga	142	519	90	145	30	7	29	101	.279	134	298	31	.933
1957	Washington	9	31	4	9	2	0	2	5	.290	2	16	1	.947
1958	Indianapolis	38	121	14	26	5	1	2	10	.215	28	79	11	.907
1958	Chattanooga	86	299	58	92	17	1	17	54	.308	97	134	12	.951
1958	Washington	13	31	2	6	0	0	0	2	.194	8	13	0	1.000
1959	Washington	153	546	98	132	20	2	42	105	.242	135	325	30	.939
1960	Washington	128	442	84	122	19	1	31	80	.276	629	135	17	.978
1961	Minnesota	150	541	94	156	20	7	46	122	.288	1000	142	23	.980
1962	Minnesota	155	552	85	134	21	1	48	126	.243	241	5	9	.964
1963	Minnesota	142	515	88	133	18	0	45	96	.258	219	7	3	.987
1964	Minnesota	158	577	95	156	11	1	49	111	.270	282	1	7	.971
1965	Minnesota	113	401	78	108	16	1	25	75	.269	743	113	12	.986
Major League Totals		1112	3828	651	998	131	13	297	745	.263	3262	852	111	.974

INDEX

INDEX

187

About the Author

Hal Butler was born in St. Louis, Missouri, but moved to Detroit, Michigan, as a child and has spent most of his life there. Educated in the public schools, he got his first writing experience as a reporter for his high school newspaper.

Always too much of a light-weight to actively participate in major sports, he nevertheless played most sports as a youngster and has kept close to the sport scene during his adult life. His writing career has been one of great variety for the past twenty years, including sport and detective fiction, as well as non-fiction on sports, travel, history, adventure, automobiles and general subjects. Mr. Butler's stories have appeared in *Saturday Evening Post, Coronet, Pageant, Sport, True, American Mercury* and several foreign publications.

At the present time he serves as a senior editor on the *Ford Times*, a national travel magazine published by the Ford Motor Company. He and his family live in Detroit and commute during the summer months to a log cabin in northwestern Michigan. Other than writing, Mr. Butler's favorite avocation is travel, having visited most of the continental United States, Hawaii, Europe and the Caribbean.